Beardie's World

Joyce Ives

Clink Street

London | New York

Published by Clink Street Publishing 2018

Copyright © 2018

First edition.

*The author asserts the moral right under the Copyright, Designs and Patents Act 1988 to be identified as the author of this work.
All rights reserved. No part of this publication may be reproduced, stored in a retrieval system or transmitted, in any form or by any means without the prior consent of the author, nor be otherwise circulated in any form of binding or cover other than that with which it is published and without a similar condition being imposed on the subsequent purchaser.*

*ISBN: 978-1-912562-27-5 paperback
978-1-912562-28-2 ebook*

ACKNOWLEDGEMENTS

I would like to thank my husband John for all his patience; my grandson Connor for proof reading; my son Duncan and grandson Jordan for their computer help; all giving up their precious time and encouraging me.

THE RAINBOW BRIDGE

There is a bridge connecting Heaven and Earth. It is called The Rainbow Bridge because of its many colours. Just this side of the bridge there is a land of meadows, hills and valleys with lush green grass.

When a beloved pet dies it goes to this place. There is always food and water and warm spring weather. The old and frail animals are made young again, those who are maimed are made whole again. They play all day with each other. There is only one thing missing – their special guardians who loved them on Earth.

Each day they run and play until finally the day comes when one pet suddenly stops playing and looks up. The nose twitches. The ears come up and it suddenly breaks away from the group. You have been seen and when you and your beloved friend meet, you take them into your arms and embrace. Your face is kissed again and again and again and you look once more into the eyes of your pet.

Then you cross the bridge together, never again to be apart.

Joyce Ives

JUNE 1986 – THE BEGINNING

What was happening to me? I felt myself being pushed along in a steady rhythm, unsure whether I liked this feeling. I was moist and warm and suddenly I was ejected from my comfort zone and found myself lying among other bodies making lots of high pitched squeaking. Strange smells all around me, I had a rough tongue rapidly pushing my body about, licking and licking me clean and dry. I too emitted the same squeaking; it was bedlam, my eyes were tight shut and I had to feel my way around knocking into other little warm bodies, seven of them. The big body with the rough tongue was moving about sorting us out. I then heard a new noise, which I found out later was a human telling the big body (Mother) to lie down. A large hand picked us up one by one and we were put against our Mother's teats, snuggling amongst the long hair trying to latch on for our first feed.

Several weeks have passed and we were plump and very furry, two were brown and the rest of us were slate. Our eyes were now open and we were now able to walk. Whenever our Mother settled down amongst us it was a mad fight to find the best teat to suck the most delicious milk and my larger siblings could actually latch on when our milk bar was standing.

We all enjoyed finding the brightest parts in our outside pen basking in the sunlight, although sometimes, looking up, there were blobs of white moving across the blue sky. Usually we huddled together during our sleep time to keep warm. During this time we were visited by large faces staring down at us and smaller faces with tender smiles, laughing at our antics as we played together. Each face gave out a different sound as their mouths moved. One larger face came often and I started to recognise the sound and looked forward to her coming and giving me extra cuddles, burying her face in my fur. I think she is going to call me Kizzy.

At seven weeks old I was the first to leave my birth Mother when the same lady came and carried me away. I felt a pang of regret leaving my brothers and sisters – we had had such fun together – now I was on my own for the first time. Everything smelt so different, although I recognised that distinctive smell of my new Mother. It was the first time I had travelled in a moving noisy box which had round wheels, not paws like mine, and I was held close by someone I now know was Nanny, to make me feel safe. I licked her hands in gratitude and Mum smiled down at me. After what seemed like a long journey I was carried into a building which was to be my new home and then straight out into the garden. Trembling, I hid behind the flower pots and refused to go into the big house as I was a bit frightened. A large man came out to see me; I knew it was a man as he smelt totally different to Mum. He picked me up and in a deep booming voice said, "So this is Kizzy! What a beautiful Bearded Collie puppy." He was to be my Dad. I was shown my new sleeping accommodation in the conservatory and immediately crawled into a comfy box under a bench which was nice and dark. Meanwhile, I found it rather strange as I watched Mum placing rustling white stuff with black patterns down on the concrete. During the night I used these to pee on, but was worried that Dad might be cross because I had seen him sitting quietly examining each sheet. Well, he would not be able to read them now. The next morning I was praised for not crying for my siblings.

For the first week in my new home I was driven to Nanny's. This involved sitting in my bean bag at the back of Mum's car

Joyce Ives

for a ten minute ride whilst Mum worked in the mornings to earn money to feed me. I decided I liked this new life with all the cuddles and attention. As I was so good at Nanny's it was decided that I could stay at home with the garden to play in, but being young I spent most of my time sleeping while Mum was absent.

As soon as my injections were completed, I was allowed out into the New World to face the hustle and bustle which I found very exciting. New smells, monster cars flashing by, and meeting other dogs who were also wearing collars attached to leads walking along with their owners. Mum had great delight in telling her friends I wasn't pulling on my lead because we had practised in the garden.

My next new frightening experience was Training School. The hall echoed with young barking puppies scrabbling their paws along the wooden floor in their enthusiasm to say hello to all their new friends. I was allowed to join in for a while before the teacher clapped her hands to begin our education to obey commands and learn how to behave. I was so good it wasn't long before we moved into the Big Dogs' Class.

Time rolled by so happily. I eventually learned that I had to keep still when lifted onto an old kitchen table whilst Mum groomed me. She cleaned my ears and teeth once a week. I was a terrible fidget and tried Mum's patience many times by jumping down with Mum in hot pursuit chasing me around the garden. Autumn arrived and it was great fun chasing falling leaves and experiencing for the first time the damp odour as we walked through the woods. Snow fell and I loved rolling in it, although I hated it when it turned into ice balls between my toes and I had difficulty walking. At night I snuggled lower in my bean bag as it got colder. One evening, while lying cosily on the lounge carpet, television broadcasts kept mentioning about not leaving animals out in the extreme cold, so I was surprised when I was left in the kitchen at night. That was real luxury for me!

However, the weather soon warmed up again, although I did keep hearing, "When is summer coming?"

I found it quite hot some days and dug a nice big hole under a bush in the garden to lie and keep cool in. Mum muttered something about her not minding as long as this was the only one.

One work day morning when instead of being told, "Be a good girl, Mummy won't be long," my Mum took me to her office. I soon got used to the noisy typewriter as I slept under her desk and loved the extra fuss I received from Mum's work colleagues. In the lunch hour I was allowed to dash about in different woods and fields and even managed to catch a young squirrel under my paw and was a bit miffed when Mum made me let it go. This lovely new socialising experience only lasted two weeks as Mum was covering for someone who had gone on holiday.

A month or so later, a visit to North Wales was mentioned and all of us going on holiday there. Mum had a friend who had set up a bed and breakfast and they were allowed to take me. What Mum said next had me sitting bolt upright. Was I hearing correctly? When we get back we would be having a new puppy! At last, I had got my way, because every time I was exercised in large park areas, I always rushed up to play with any dog that was about. Of course I soon tired them out, and I came back to Mum always telling her that I really needed a playmate of my own.

We left for Wales and I had the longest car ride ever. We kept stopping for comfort breaks for me and of course them. Mum was pleased with me and kept telling Dad how laid back I was. Whatever that means.

At our B & B I slept in Mum and Dad's bedroom. Of course I was on my best behaviour; the owners had a farm dog called Fred, not a pedigree like me, he was half German Shepherd half Samoyed, and slept outside in a wooden kennel. I suppose he was used to it. He was such good fun and we shared my first experience of sand and sea, including chasing seagulls. I ate crab legs which was nice and salty but my stomach didn't care for it! My week's holiday was so exciting; car rides, mountain walks, waterfalls and streams, and don't I love water. I must have been the cleanest dog in Wales that week.

Home again and after a good night's sleep I woke up to find Mum bustling about making up my old box with new bedding and being told I was going to have a playmate called Emma. Later I sat up in amazement when this tiny fawn and white furry creature gambolled through the conservatory and out into MY garden. I was told she was a baby Beardie and that I was to be kind to her.

Well, I did as I was told, as I am grown up now and have to set a good example at thirteen months old. I allowed her to sleep in my bean bag (I found her box rather small as my tail had to hang out), eat from my bowl as well as her own, and take toys from my mouth. She was reprimanded though when hanging onto my collar for grim death. When she pulls out mouthfuls of my fur, I thump her with my paw, but then I feel sorry as I don't mean to hurt her and run guiltily to my Mum for sympathy.

Walks now include the three of us, with Emma inside a shoulder bag zipped up with just her head out so she gets used to traffic whizzing by and is safe. When we get back I am not happy having my face and paws washed in disinfectant, though I am told it will not last forever – until Emma has had her vaccinations.

When Emma is asleep, Mum plays with me, but I often lie down thoughtfully wondering how next year will pan out as Emma grows up and we do more and more things together. We shall have to wait and see.

KIZZY

1988 – LIFE WITH EMMA

I have decided to keep a diary so that in my veteran years with the help of Mum I can look back on all the adventures and trials and tribulations that Emma and me, Kizzy, have experienced together, and whoever reads this will enter into our Canine World.

Some eighteen months have now passed and a lot has happened since my little fawn sister joined our family. Emma is still quite a handful and Mum said she is a typical Beardie, so what does that make me? I am really proud to write our journal, this is the difference between Emma and me. Emma couldn't write a journal; she can't keep still for more than five minutes, although, upon reflection, she is quite vocal!

To continue… Just before she was allowed down on the ground, we were out on one of our lovely walks. I was rushing on ahead across the fields and Mum was staggering along with Emma as she was now quite heavy, when to my great surprise my little playmate shot passed me. Oh great joy! Emma had wriggled out of Mum's shoulder bag. With the wind blowing through our coats, we flew happily across the first field like a couple of tornadoes. I did hear hysterical screaming which quickly faded, and all we could hear was each other panting as we reached the third field. I turned and remembered Mum, I could see an outline of her way up on the hill; no way! She was running away from us, not chasing us, so I led the way this time and hi-tailed it back with Emma in hot pursuit. Mum was really pleased to see us, Emma was whisked up and popped back into the shoulder bag and I was given a titbit for being such a good girl! This was a taste of things to come.

At the beginning of 1988, Mum decided that our sleeping accommodation needed to be more comfortable and luxurious, to be in keeping with Beardies like us. She persuaded Dad to have our house all knocked down. At the time we were not at all happy our home had gone and we had to sleep indoors, but when we saw our new surroundings, well we felt like a couple of toffs. Double glazed roof, windows and door. Tiled floor – not concrete – and a radiator for the really cold weather. We shared it with a few plants and our two tortoises who rarely speak to us – not at all in the winter as they are tucked up in a big box of straw. In the summer they are just a couple of meat pies on legs but not at all tasty. Anyway, our conservatory home is brilliant, even if we did hear Dad grumble to Mum that, "Those two dogs are costing more than I expected."

Summer was very memorable. Emma helped me dig an even larger hole under my favourite bush, and even helped Mum dig holes for the bedding plants. I taught her how to drink out of the bird bath, but, being the madcap she is (she goes overboard in everything she does), she managed to knock the water bowl off and break the stone base. We also turned the garden, which is Mum's favourite hobby (second to us of course), into a race track; there was no lawn left to mow and the mature azaleas were just stumps sticking out of the ground which made good chewing sticks for us. The neighbours shook their heads in disbelief when looking over the fence and said that the garden couldn't be entered into the local competition for 'Prettiest Garden' anymore.

AFTER PLAYING CHASE IN THE GARDEN

A great heated discussion ensued between Mum and Dad about how one Beardie was fine, but two were a disaster. At this point we got really worried and kept trying to climb on their laps telling them that we wouldn't put so much effort in trying to race one another and maybe the grass would start to grow again and of course they could buy some new plants, couldn't they?

We were even more worried when we spent a couple of confusing weeks being kept out of the garden as we listened to cement mixers and squeaking wheelbarrows and observed from the dining room total disorder and chaos, which was far more than we had caused. Strange men extended the patio and erected wrought iron railings with a gate at the end of it. One of Mum's Beardie friends was sure that it was not high enough and certainly wouldn't contain her Beardies, but once we were allowed into our new 'clean' area, we never thought to jump the railings. No of course not, but Emma being Emma squeezed through the gaps. She wasn't going to be stopped going under her favourite bush. The trouble was, she couldn't get back, so was always barking for the gate to be opened. Another prevention job for Dad.

LET ME OUT I PROMISE TO BE GOOD

Now she is more mature, she can't get through, and quite honestly we all seem happy with the situation. Mum can dig her garden without Emma helping her, and Dad is pleased that in the past year the garden has returned to normal. What he wasn't pleased about was the cost, but when he is asleep in the chair and we wake him up with a big slobbery kiss, we know he has forgiven us.

Here is something else which will make you laugh; when it rains and is muddy my Mum puts me in a waterproof coat; Emma was told she had to finish growing before she could have one, so I always feel special when I wear it. Unfortunately one rainy day we both decided to jump in the river and I forgot I was special. Mum said I looked like the Michelin Man when I staggered out of the water. Needless to say, I'm not allowed to wear it when going on rainy river walks.

As Emma got older Mum took on a new hobby called 'showing'. On the day of Emma's first show, Emma was allowed to wear MY coat on our early morning walk AND she wore BEARDIE BOOTS! I was so jealous. The coat was too big for her and she looked stupid, so I dived into her, rolled her over, cuffing her ears. After I had had my say, she picked herself up. One boot was off, she had a dirty head and one of her front paws was sticking through the neck piece. That taught her to be so high-and-mighty, and when they got back from the show Emma told me she hadn't even been placed!

She has of course since then been placed many times, including eight firsts, and also won a big cup for Best in Show at Wycombe. She strutted around showing off for days.

We were very lucky this year, because Dad said we had cost him such a lot of money, he and Mum couldn't have an expensive holiday, so they took us on two walking holidays. One in Yorkshire in July where we had a super time getting wet in the water and out as it rained all week. We didn't mind a bit but I think Mum and Dad did. Thank goodness the accommodation had a tumble dryer for our towels.

In October we spent the second week at the Braddabrooks' house, a lady breeder who had lots and lots of Beardies. The weather was kind to us and we had even better walks. It helped being able to see where we were going. Mum and Dad kept dry, but we didn't. Emma came into season and the breeder named her 'the High Wycombe Harlot'; typical Emma, she is always so pushy. The poor rampant boy Beardies had to be shut out and Emma kept asking to join them. I thought she was MY friend. She has no finesse, not like me!

Next year Mum and Dad are going abroad. Dad says he wants a 'quiet' holiday, sunshine and sand, so kennels have been mentioned. I have only stayed at that unmentionable place once and it was so long ago I can't remember what it was like. Still, I'll have my bouncy friend Emma with me this time and I am sure we will survive.

I know it was good for Mum and Dad to get me a little sister. We get on very well together, but I do get fed up sometimes when she continually dive bombs me. Maybe Mum will get another Beardie puppy and perhaps the new one will dive bomb Emma and leave me in peace. Well that's worth dreaming about!

1989 – MORE 'TAILS' FROM KIZZY

We are off on another trip today, but I understand this time it is to the Bankruptcy Court!

Dad is muttering about how he had to double glaze the conservatory to provide us with extra warmth, extend and put railings up on the patio to keep us off the garden and now he sighs that Mum's car isn't big enough to take us both… Emma and I feel like princesses in our nearly new Nissan Prairie, quite a step up from the Ford Fiesta.

Well, 1989 has proved quite a disastrous year for us and the year hasn't ended yet! Both Emma and I are very well known at our vets and Mum is more than pleased with PetPlan Insurance.

Towards the end of last year, I started to scratch and scratch and scratch. The visits to the vet went from once a week to every other day. It was my diet, they said. It was a food allergy. After weeks of being on boiled lamb and rice, I was so unhappy. I suffered pills, injections and creams. I had chewed my back legs until they were raw and Mum had to bandage them. My ears were constantly quivering and I felt so degraded when I had to wear a plastic lampshade to protect my head and ears. When Mum had spare moments, she sat on the floor to cuddle me trying to calm me down. I was so depressed; Emma wanted to play but I was too ill and crept away in a corner to get away from everybody.

Three months passed with almost daily visits to the vets, we were told it wasn't catching so Emma was still going to shows. After seeing five vets at our practice, no-one knew what was wrong with me. Mum almost in tears demanded to see a specialist and as the London Veterinary College was fully booked for two months we got an immediate appointment to see a skin specialist in Coventry. I slept on the back seat of Dad's car (normally taboo) lying upside down with the horrible lampshade on. By this time, Emma had started to scratch too but our vet said Mum was getting neurotic and there was nothing wrong with her apart from her anal glands, which they emptied!

Arriving at the specialist I weakly tried to climb up on the table I had climbed so many times, but the kind man wanted to interview Mum and Dad first asking them lots of questions about me and then the final question was asked: had THEY any bites or a rash? Mum's mouth dropped open when Dad bared his chest revealing a rash which had only come up the night before. The specialist took a scraping of skin from inside my ear flap and disappeared into his laboratory reappearing five minutes later with a big smile and invited Mum and Dad to look down his microscope. SARCOPTIC MANGE – what a relief to get a diagnosis! Little did I realise what was ahead for Emma and I, and even Mum and Dad!

We had to be bathed in Quellada every week, and it took nearly three months before we finally got rid of our terrible itching. We were so fed up and disappeared every time the bath was run, but Emma and I did get a laugh at the beginning of the treatment when Mum and Dad had to stand naked and shivering in the bathroom for five minutes before they could shower off the Quellada they had applied to each other's bodies. They only had to have three applications and each time they were in the bathroom there were heated discussions on the 'joys' of owning dogs! They never discussed how we felt, we lost count how many times we were tempted into the bathroom with tasty snacks waved in front of our noses.

Beardies World

At last we were cleared of carrying those microscopic mites – sighs of relief all round, now we could socialise with our Beardie friends again.

The next disaster was when Mum, Emma and I were saying goodbye to Adele (Mum and Dad's daughter) at the front door. It was cold and snowing and Mum pulled the inner hall door closed to keep the heat in. Emma screamed and we all thought Mum had caught her paw, but as Emma moved away, blood shot around the walls of the porch and when Mum reopened the inner door, the end of Emma's tail was stuck to the hinged side of the door!

Panic reigned as Emma was quickly scooped up and with her tail hurriedly bandaged we raced off in the car to the vets. I assessed the stressful situation and quietly sniffed at Emma sitting on Adele's lap to try and pacify her. Also looking over Mum's shoulder as she was driving along, I saw the end of Emma's tail laid across Mum's legs. I leaned forward to lick Mum's salty tears away so she could see where she was driving and we arrived at the vets without any more mishaps. Poor Emma, she was very nervous for quite a while whilst the vet examined her and said the end of her beautiful tail couldn't be sewn back on. We picked her up later after the vet had to cut more of her tail off so he could pull the skin over the end of her injury. She cringed every time she wagged her tail and hit it against something until it had fully healed.

The Kennel Club wrote to Mum saying that Emma can be shown and sent a letter that was to be handed to the steward before they went in the ring, so now the fur has regrown over the injured end of her tail Mum is going to try showing her again (good luck Emma).

Other visits to the vets have been to have our badly cut paws stitched. We live in an area which is very flinty, and Mum tries to keep us away from these areas now. Vet fees since Mum joined PetPlan have been over £500 and that is only in the last eighteen months. I was back at the vets just recently and told I can't have puppies. I would have liked to have a family but Mum said my mouth is overshot and I mustn't pass the defect on. I had to be kept on my lead for ten days, which annoyed Emma who constantly barked at me to play and run with her. Mum got the worst of it because, when we were in the woods, I dragged her through the undergrowth to sniff at all the special smells. Not only did she have to pick the sweetheart burrs out of my coat but also needed to pick the broken branches out of her hair and clothes.

At the time of writing this, our last visit to the vets was for our annual injections and Timmy tortoise came too as he had a cold and wasn't well. He had to have two injections, antibiotics and multivitamins. He is a little better, but still a bit snuffly.

What is happening to the Ives' household? Even Dad ended up in hospital for three days on a drip. He had food poisoning. I tried to tell Mum that if he ate the same as us girls for dinner he wouldn't have been ill.

Mum and Dad had their sunshine and sea holiday. Why they had to go abroad when England was just as hot I don't know, but we were duly packed off to the 'dreaded kennels'. We had been given a trial run of two days to get us used to it. I thought, "I will teach Mum a lesson," and held myself for two days. The trouble was, it was me who was uncomfortable. On staying there a fortnight, the nice kennel lady was asked to keep an eye on me. I held myself again: Emma told me not to be so silly, but I was surprised when I was taken out on my lead and still I wouldn't perform. Then Emma was brought along for company, but still I refused to go. By the third day I was put in a paddock on my own, let off the lead and told to do my 'two twos'. What on earth was that lady talking about? My Mum always said 'hurry up' or 'quickly' to me when she wanted me to function. I just stared at the lady and she stomped out mumbling to herself how stubborn Beardies can be. When I thought no one was watching me I relieved myself. I can't help it if Mum abandons me, I'm more sensitive about these personal things than Emma.

The Southern Counties Bearded Collie Club hold three fun events a year. The Spring Frolic, Strawberry Tea and the Tramps Tuck-In. It was September and we travelled to another breeder's home; they kept greyhounds as well as Beardies, and there was a huge running track which we all charged around chasing one another. I have never seen so many Beardies together all enjoying themselves, I had fun flirting with the boy Beardies too. Of course the two legged owners were tucking into their tea, but all we managed to tuck into was the baked bean juice off the paper plates. I noticed some Beardies were given pieces of sausage but no such luck for us.

We both failed our Junior Working Tests, but that was not our fault – Mum hadn't trained us properly. I refused point blank to fetch the dumbbell. (It is a silly game anyway.) Emma showed willing but either spat the dumbbell out, or brought it back to Mum but hung onto it for grim death and wouldn't let it go!

I did win the Musical Sits. Emma went out in the last ten, because she lost her concentration. The most exciting part of the day was us actually meeting the Supreme Champion, Cassie, and seeing that enormous cup which she won at Crufts.

As this year hasn't been a good year for the Ives Beardies and humans, we are hoping for a change in our fortunes. In late September we leave for an adventure holiday on Dartmoor with our doggy friend Noah. He is crossed between a little black poodle and a Wheaten Terrier. He has his dad's golden colour and his mum's curly coat. A very handsome lad, but not at all intelligent like us. It should be fun as there are going to be six human friends coming with us.

1990 – KIZZY – THE TRUTH 'PENNED' BY EMMA

Kizzy thinks she is so clever writing stories about our adventures and struts about with her nose in the air; she never lets me, Emma, forget how famous we are becoming, all because of her putting paw to paper. Well, enough is enough and I feel it's about time I let you know a few home truths to put her in her place!

What about the time when…

She was a puppy and buried a bone with her nose and got an infection up her nasal passages and ended up at the vets having her nose irrigated and her head X-rayed to make sure a small stone hadn't got stuck.

What about the time when…

She thought she was like the Labrador puppy on the television and enjoyed unravelling the toilet roll and happily trailed it around the house.

What about the time when…

She was naughty being groomed, and Dad had to sit by the grooming table to talk to her and hold her down if a knot was found while Mum worked on carefully removing it.

What about the time when…

A Rottweiler attacked her and knocked Mum over and **I** had to do my protection bit and chase it away.

What about the time when…

Mum put us on a diet and Kizzy stole twelve frozen sausages

off of Nanny's kitchen table. It was a wonder we couldn't hear them rattling in her stomach.

What about the time when…

She buried her bone in a tray of Alyssum, ploughing through the seed boxes of Tagettes and Salvia that were on the patio hardening off. Mum was not amused at the devastation.

What about the time when…

We visited pro dog houses and Mum had to ask the owners to shut their bathroom doors to stop Kizzy jumping in their baths and unravelling their toilet rolls. Anyone that knew her fetish and saw us coming rushed to shut the bathroom door before letting us in!

Beardies World

Finally, what about the time when…

One morning Auntie Ginny, who had two Beardie girls like us called Ailsa and Staffa, kindly took us all on a new woodland walk. It was summer time and we travelled there in her brand new estate car which was sweet smelling and nice and shiny. We all had a lovely time exploring together, it was wonderful investigating new smells but all good things come to an end and we started to return to the car. Kizzy's nose pointed skyward, sniffing the air, and she shot off in the direction of an almost dried up pond. The birds took flight when Mum yelled, "Down Kizzy, down!" Well, Kizzy stopped and dropped like a stone about a yard from the edge of the foul smelling liquid. Mum raced towards her – wow, this looked like fun – and I bounced over to investigate the drama; I overtook Mum, shot past Kizzy and ended up to my neck in a most extraordinary substance. Naturally, as Mum had forgotten the command word 'stay', Kizzy joined me, doing her favourite impression of a hippo.

Auntie Ginny put Ailsa and Staffa on the back seats to keep them away from us and we sat in the back; the car had lost its nice and fresh smell. Once home, we were left feeling pretty uncomfortable as Mum had to go straight to work and left us out in the garden. The slime, leaf mould, bits of sticks and weeds dried, making us look like giant hedgehogs. On her return, Mum staggered upstairs, carrying us one at a time into the bathroom. She wanted us respectable before Dad arrived home from his office.

What a performance. Mum changed into her bikini and we were put in the shower, then across to the bath, back to the shower. It was endless going to and fro; we felt she was overdoing it a bit. Surely we must have been clean by now? Dad got home just as we were shaking ourselves, spraying leaf mould bits over the bathroom floor and tiles, clogging the grouting. Our seething Dad carried us downstairs and once again we were shut outside.

We were not used to such unloving treatment. Usually Mum dried us off immediately after a bath. Our noses were pressed against the patio window as we watched them eat their dinner, which Dad had cooked. What about our dinner? Whilst Dad washed up, Mum disappeared upstairs to try to clean the bathroom. After hearing what trouble we were in, Auntie Barbara, another friend, arrived to see for herself, making a mental note that her next puppy would not be a Beardie. It was just as well she came because she helped Dad pick Mum up off the bathroom floor. We were not sure why Mum was doing aerobics, or was it yoga? She managed to slip in the shower and get her right leg twisted backwards behind her neck.

The unloving treatment continued; were we to be ignored? What about our dinner? The doctor was called, then a big white van arrived with a flashing light. We could hear the strange men who went upstairs. Looking up at the window we saw them peering down at us it was all rather confusing. There was a lot of laughing and joking. Mind you, we couldn't hear Dad; Mum was the noisiest, something about administering laughing gas so they could get her down the stairs into the white van. When they left at 9.30pm Mum was still wearing her bikini and we still hadn't been fed!

I heaved a big sigh and stared at Kizzy, wishing she hadn't smelt that water. Look at the trouble she had got us into! We were both still wet and miserable with rumbling tums. How dare Mum get all the attention. I know she's our boss, but how can she be our leader with a suspected broken hip?

OH DEAR, DO YOU THINK MUM AND DAD WILL FORGIVE US!

We found out later when our bowls were eventually placed before us at midnight that Mum's hip had only momentarily dislocated but had popped back into its socket again. No problem, all was well, or so we thought.

Our lives for the next four weeks were certainly different. Dad walked us in the mornings and evenings and in the afternoons; a rota was organised and several of Mum's Beardie friends, including Auntie Barbara who loves us dearly, came and took us out. Of course I told Kizzy to be on her best behaviour during this time. Unfortunately, on one of our afternoon walks, Kizzy again smelt water. The Good Samaritan on that particular day arriving back splattered in mud, protesting she had no idea that there was a pond behind the hedge where she had walked us. Her Beardies of course didn't like water so didn't follow us. We regretted our behaviour once again and this time the hose was unkindly turned on us.

Oh Kizzy, why do your amphibious tendencies always get us into trouble? We didn't think we would see our Good Samaritan again, but a couple of days later she returned determined that she wasn't going to be beaten by a couple of unruly Beardies!

I have exposed the real Kizzy, but she is my best friend and I always leave her a tasty bit of dinner in the bottom of my bowl as she has manners and waits patiently for me to finish.

Writing this was hard work as I am thirteen months younger than Kizzy, so I will leave the continuation of our diary to Kizzy in future.

KIZZY AND EMMA HAVING FUN

1991 – OBEDIENCE OR DISOBEDIENCE? 'PENNED' BY KIZZY

Mum has been training us for obedience competitions (more like disobedience considering our past record – she's got no chance). This obedience lark has happened because our canine family was going to increase with another baby sister joining us, but we were told we would have to wait a little longer, so Mum felt she should use the time to try to instil some sense into us. She wants her next Beardie to be an angel – a Hell's Angel if she is to fit in here. Emma and I were taken regularly to our local Obedience Club as we had a couple of competitions to enter.

The one at Ipswich was a disaster for me: I was doing really well, then was disqualified for doing the unmentionable in the ring. Mum had taken me again and again to the exercise area, but as I have told you before I have to have privacy; then, I couldn't hold it any longer, assumed the position and really was in disgrace. Emma came seventh, and of course wasn't in the line-up to receive a rosette. The next competition at Langford was an anti-climax as Mum wasn't well, so we were not allowed to go.

One of our neighbours who lived across the road was very interested to hear that us Beardies kept a diary and asked to read it. She was a school teacher at St. Bernard's Preparatory School in Slough and decided to read our diary to her class as part of the school's Book Week. After listening to them, they were asked to draw a picture and write about our adventures.

We were surprised to be invited to attend the school to see all the stories and pictures on the walls and meet the thirty-five children. Mum's daughter Adele came too to hold either one of us as we were each put through our paces showing heel work, sit, stay and lie down. The children were very quiet and well behaved, sitting cross-legged on the floor watching us, and when we had finished they all clapped.

Each little child was invited to say hello, but several were terrified, backing away, saying they didn't like dogs, but when they saw everyone else stroking and cuddling us, they forgot their fears and came forward not to be left out.

A few days later, the postman delivered a big envelope. Inside there were thirty-five letters from the children thanking us and saying how much they enjoyed our visit, with lots more drawings. We were so proud and Mum put our thank you letters on the wall in our conservatory.

The rest of the year was pretty dull (for us, that is); we had the usual two weeks in kennels, the odd show here and there, but did enjoy a long weekend staying with one of Dad's friends up in Ulverston (Lake District). We were warned to be on our best behaviour as this family had never had dogs in their house before and were not doggy people at all, so why we were invited we were not sure. Was it curiosity to see what Beardies were like?

On arrival we settled in straight away but Emma took it a bit too far, barking madly at the mistress of the house when she came home from work, walking in through the back door. We hadn't met her up until then and Emma was protecting us. Oh dear, this wasn't a good start. The only other incident was up Coniston Old Man Mountain, when Emma took off after a sheep, dragging Joanne, one of our host's siblings, down the mountain with Dad shouting, "Don't let her go!" with no thought for Joanne's safety.

Guess what, we were actually told we could visit again, even with a third Beardie! Mum and Dad drove us home, proud of us.

Events did 'hot up' during the summer. Have any of you had trouble with farmers? Well, we have! Mum and Dad's group of friends decided to go on one of their periodic walks; we should have known from the start that it would be one of those days. At the very beginning of the walk we somehow managed to knock off and break one of the walker's expensive spectacles. Thank goodness for Petplan (Mum and Dad were presented with a bill for £270 a few days later).

Following this incident, much to our amazement, we were kept on the lead, but as we neared the Halfway House pub, Mum decided that as the crops had been harvested we could be let off for a short run. Unbeknown to her, but obviously not to us with our keen sense of smell, there was something far better than a ploughman's lunch waiting. We both found 'it' together.

A huge morass of rotting and fermenting marrows and cabbages. I just left my calling card – all you could see of Emma was her four legs flailing ecstatically skywards! Up until this point the walk had been a peaceful, pleasant stroll in the countryside. The sight of a not-so-fawn Beardie covered in evil-smelling black slime, with the walkers just ten minutes away from sustenance, was enough to put a damper on the proceedings.

With fear and trepidation (Dad was nowhere to be seen, he was too embarrassed), Mum approached the farmer whose field we were walking through to request the use of a hosepipe. His immediate reaction and words of advice offered were not printable, but translated went something like this. "Oh goodness, what a smelly dog, would you like some water, my dear, to wash it?"

After a haggle, he relented and took Mum, Emma and a couple of our walkers to a nearby shed where an old large fire hose lay outside on the dusty ground. He disappeared, obviously to turn on the water. He turned the hose pipe on full blast, which made it snake gushing water all over the place. By the look on the farmer's face it looked as though he meant it to happen.

His smile rapidly turned to dismay when he saw the hose was depositing water into the open window of his car and in turn spraying all of us, including him. With the hose eventually under control, and Emma held at arm's length, she was cleaned up sufficiently for us to adjourn to the pub. Naturally enough, we had to eat outside. Following a scrumptious lunch, not enhanced by Emma's body odour, the return journey was uneventful, but just to even things up I found my usual bog, the only time again we were let off the lead. We try so hard to please Mum and Dad, but the desire for our own special perfume seems to make us deaf to our pack leader's commands. I don't understand why Mum wants to take us to obedience classes, do you?

Joyce Ives

OUR INTRODUCTION TO DARTMOOR

The end of September arrived, and to our horror the suitcases were brought down from their storage area. Dad had disappeared through a hole in the ceiling! We have never seen what is up there. Surely our two legged owners were not leaving us again? We hadn't heard mention of kennels, but then we were told, "Yes, you are coming too," so I didn't lie in the open suitcase this time to stop clothes being put in.

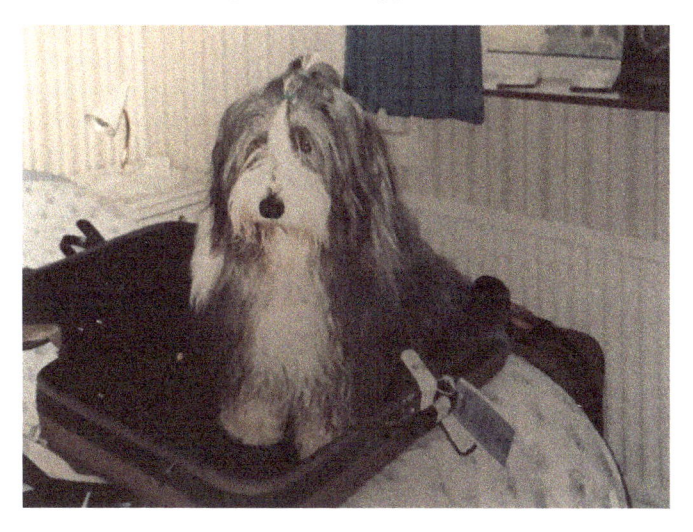

THIS IS WHAT I DO WHEN WE ARE NOT ALLOWED TO GO!

Our dogmobile was packed the previous evening, which I supervised, while Emma hid behind the settee. After making sure OUR beanbags were in the back, I promptly sat on them and stayed there whilst Mum and Dad struggled out with boxes of OUR food, towels, sheeting, and bowl for washing our paws in. Dad wanted to know, as a washing up bowl had been packed – why not take the kitchen sink as well! Then came the boxes of THEIR food, suitcases, walking sticks, etc. Thank goodness Mum had changed her car. After quite a bit of pleading from Mum, I was coaxed out of the car. I still felt they might leave us at home, so I joined Emma behind the settee.

The next morning after meeting with Mum & Dad's other friends and our veteran friend Noah (he was given that name because he did lots of puddles when he was a puppy), we set off on our next adventure.

It was a three hour car ride stopping on the way at a place called Stonehenge, but we were not allowed to see it as NO DOGS signs were up. However, there was an area we were allowed to run, so we missed being educated on the pile of stones on the opposite side of the road.

We were quivering with excitement when we arrived at our holiday home in North Bovey, Dartmoor. While Dad waited for the key, Mum took us and Noah for a short walk. There was a field nearby and Mum walked us towards it. Suddenly a woman called to us saying, "Don't let your dogs do their 'business' in that field because my horses will roll in it and it's awful to get off!" What a strange lady! We don't object to rolling in horses' dung: we think it's wonderful and the wetter and smellier the better.

The owner of the holiday barn, when seeing Emma and me, was rather shocked and said, "Goodness, what about my carpets?" But everyone assured her that thick dustsheets would be put down in the entrance hall. Mum produced the bowl our paws are washed in and if we were really wet and smelly, we had to stay in the car until we dried off. For one terrible moment, we thought we were not going to be allowed indoors even though Mum had paid extra money for us to stay. We sat perfectly still and put our 'good as gold' faces on, which convinced the owner to say, "Yes it's alright."

Once indoors, we explored every nook and cranny of the beautiful converted barn. The lounge upstairs had an off-white carpet and we found this door always firmly closed unless everyone decided to sit in there. The bedrooms were off limits, no dogs allowed. ('Everyone' was Mum and Dad, Barbara and Michael, Wendy and Aly.) The kitchen was the size of our own lounge and dining room and this was to be our sleeping accommodation. Noah, however, had other ideas: when we were put to bed, he whined, howled and barked. We couldn't bear it and hid under the dining room table until eventually Barbara, after much scolding, took the poor old senile veteran of twelve years into their bedroom. Peace at last!

The very first new noises to greet us the next morning were a cockerel crowing, chickens scratching about outside and the horses being brought into the courtyard to be groomed before being exercised.

Now strangely enough we hadn't been warned that Mum and Dad's other friends, Wendy and Aly, were not at all doggy-minded and that the big man Aly was actually frightened of dogs! How brave to come away with us. If we had known this, we wouldn't have greeted Wendy with our best Beardie leaps as she walked into the kitchen to make Aly a cup of tea. We thought she was going to take us for our walk, but we have learned that nighties and dressing gowns are not walking attire. We found out later that Aly makes the tea, but as he was so frightened of us he had sent Wendy instead.

Mum was soon down to take us out for a quick wee and immediately reprimanded us for chasing the chickens. We found a river a couple of minutes away and threw ourselves in it to have our early morning wash. Naturally enough we had to be dried down to be allowed indoors again. Every day after breakfast, the backpacks were filled, including delicious snacks for us and then we were off. The men took it in turns to map-read and we raced on following the most exciting smells with Noah trying to keep up with us. Once as the two-legs were arguing which was the correct direction to go, I managed to find the dirtiest cattle trough to wallow in. Wendy and Aly were gradually educated on what it is like to live with dogs, especially ones whose first love is water.

The only thing which marred my holiday was that we often walked through fields that had huge beasts grazing on the grass called cows. I was petrified. Everyone laughed at me as I am supposed to be a 'cattle dog'. Emma being Emma wasn't at all bothered and kept telling me I was silly as I kept choking on my collar trying to get out of the field. Even Aly tried to pacify me. It was confusing as the ratios were wrong. Aly was frightened of me although I am smaller than him, so surely I am entitled to be frightened of monster cows that are bigger than me?

Emma's worst moment was when she ran through a thicket chasing a rabbit and got her head covered in burrs and stumbled about because she couldn't see. She slowly found her way back to our group by smelling where we were. Everyone crowded round her and she sat very patiently, kept calm by being stroked and soothed while the burrs were worked out of her fur, breaking up into tiny little hooks. It took over fifteen minutes. Once completely free of those terrible things she was able to see again and the three of us bounced off to explore.

Noah of course couldn't always keep up with us so spent most of his time at the heels of his master and mistress. Once he was even given a day off and taken to the seaside as his back pads had swollen up and he looked as though he had high heels on.

I must tell you about one of our adventure walks. The two-legs had decided to go on a long hike across Dartmoor; the weather was so good on the holiday that the warning in the Ordnance Survey book about not taking this walk if the weather was bad didn't apply. It was a very long walk, nearly six hours, but the highlight for us was when we reached the mentioned boggy bit. Instead of us floundering and wallowing in the mud Emma and I were put on our leads to move away from it. However, Noah's Mum, Barbara, decided she didn't want to take the long way round the bog where it was dry, she wanted to go through the middle. "Come on," she shouted, "this way! It looks fine," and jumped onto what she thought was firm ground. A lasting memory will be of our friend, camera held aloft, gradually sinking into the mire. Even the humans laughed at the sight of a bedraggled Barbara dripping with slime, but triumphant that her camera was unscathed. The rest of us took the longer, drier route. Our holiday week consisted of climbing tors, throwing ourselves in smelly bogs then actually being encouraged to run through the rivers and streams to get clean again. In the evening we had a quick rest whilst everyone had hot baths, then off again to walk to the village pub for them to feed their faces. We thankfully crashed out under their tables.

The holiday was voted a great success and we are going back again in September 1990. Aly is no longer afraid of us, although he doesn't quite understand how we think and act. Perhaps after spending another week with us we will get him 'trained' to recognise our Beardie ways!

Beardies World

NOAH AFTER HE FOLLOWED BARBARA THROUGH THE BOG!

1992 – A QUIET NIGHT IN 'PENNED' BY KIZZY AND EMMA

Emma and I always know when Mum and Dad are going out: the routine changes, the bathroom looks like a sauna, cupboards and drawers open and shut and Mum has material flapping around her legs and shoes on that make a tapping noise when she walks. She even flea sprays her hair, but it has a nicer smell than the can she uses on us when we start scratching.

We wander about and then flop down and sigh, resigned to the fact that we are not included. We are stroked, given a titbit each and told: "Guard the house." Then out the door they go, the keys jangle as the door is locked, the car doors slam, the engine roars into life and Dad's car is reversed off the drive. We stand by the door listening, sigh again, walk into the lounge and sit looking at one another.

EMMA: I hate it when we are not allowed to go with them, it's such a bore guarding the house.

KIZZY: It must be somewhere they can't take us, Emma. You must admit, we are pretty lucky, it's not often we are left behind.

EMMA: Mum left us behind the fence on the patio for six weeks when she redesigned the garden last autumn.

KIZZY: Yes, but we could see her.

EMMA: As soon as we got back from our early morning walks she was out there digging up shrubs and plants and emptying all the flower beds.

KIZZY: Yes, I was really shocked when the men came and took out our eleven conifer trees. We used to play chase under those and dig holes in the summer to keep cool. I can't understand why they did it!

EMMA: I heard Mum say to the neighbours she was fed up with the roots across the lawn and the grass being dead in the summer.

KIZZY: Well I'm really unhappy because when the summer comes I will have nowhere to go because you won't let me share the bush you go under, it was mine first before you came on the scene.

EMMA: You will have to find somewhere else, that's my bush! Mum did say now the garden has been planted up mostly to shrubs, she will have more time to spend with us, because the shrubs will grow bigger and then she won't be rushing about putting bedding plants in every year. Don't forget in the spring our sleeping accommodation is turned into a greenhouse. We can hardly find room to get into our bean bags.

KIZZY: She even made our afternoon walks shorter because she wanted to get back to the garden. I hate it when she ignores us.

EMMA: Do stop moaning, Kizzy. The thing I hate most is Mum cleaning out our bedroom, it really upsets me. She tosses everything outside, our bean bags are aired, the covers are changed and she's down on her knees with a bucket and scrubbing brush.

KIZZY: Then you are in trouble when you wash her ears and jump on her back and rush in and out, dropping your toys in her bucket and barking. Why you can't lie down and keep out of her way like me, I don't know.

EMMA: Oh shut up, Basil Brush.

KIZZY: Mum is always calling me that – I wonder what she means?

EMMA: It's some old TV programme, a fox called Basil Brush. Mum calls you that because when you trot along your tail looks like Basil Brush's – straight up in the air! AND you have a goofy mouth just like his.

KIZZY: Wow, that's a bit mean of her … I thought she loved me.

EMMA: Of course she loves you, although you have embarrassed her quite a few times.

KIZZY: Like when?

EMMA: Don't you remember when you had sarcoptic mange? You were really ill and Mum got permission to take you to work with her so she could stop you scratching? None of us knew what was wrong with you at the time.

KIZZY: Yes, everyone at work laughed at me because I had that horrible big lampshade on my head. I was so miserable and sat most of the time under her desk in her posh reception area.

EMMA: Well Kizzy, what did you do to upset her?

KIZZY: Oh dear, she did have a red face that day, it was when I decided to take a wander and my lampshade got hooked up on the watering can which stood beside those beautiful plants, it was only two gallons of water across the plain royal blue carpet! Mum turned into an Olympic runner, she had a terrible time trying to mop it up. All the glue came up through the soaked carpet and it went a funny white colour. I sat in the corner thankfully having a good scratch knowing she was too busy to stop me.

EMMA: Mum was lucky not to lose her job over you and you think she doesn't love you!

KIZZY: Shhh, what's that noise? Is it burglars?

EMMA: Burglars? No one would dare, anyway Mum and Dad have just joined Neighbourhood Watch.

KIZZY: Come on, move yourself. That's the key in the door; it's Mum and Dad. Let us go and greet them. The time went really quickly, didn't it?

EMMA: Don't tell them that, let's pretend it has felt like we have been left for days.

Joyce Ives

1992 HAPPINESS IS – ELECTION DAY PROUDLY 'PENNED' BY MUFFIN

Kizzy has given me permission to make an entry into the 'Dog Diary'.

I was born on the 9th April along with my four sisters and four brothers. Neil Kinnock thought it was going to be Labour's Day, but the day belong to my mum Ailsa. Apart from Pirate, who had an odd marked face, we were named Major, Norma, Paddy, Glenys, Edwina and Dennis. I was called Maggie. We were all weighed and drawings were made of the markings we had as we were all so similar. This was the only normal and natural experience my siblings and I were to have for some time.

The first three and a half weeks of our lives were spent at Kizzy and Emma's house, as my mum's owner was away most of that time. Ailsa, tired and anxious after giving birth to us nine babies, decided she was unhappy with her accommodation. She tore open a conveniently placed sun lounger and buried us in the loose foam. Human Mum moved us back to the whelping box. She then picked us up, placing us on the grooming table. We didn't like heights and were in danger of falling off and screamed and screamed. Good heavens, this was a nightmare. Next we were all taken one by one into the garage and we were getting cold. With help from human Dad, a large roll of polythene was hastily put down in a spare room and we happily settled in there and snuggled up to our mum, feeding contentedly.

Human Mum, her name is Joyce, had a sleeping bag on the bed settee and we all calmed down for the night.

During the night, Joyce awoke to find us puppies tucked all around her and Ailsa sitting on her stomach with the expression 'you got me into this fine mess – nine puppies need to be shared – so here we are!' For the next two days and nights the settee was our home, the whelping area was empty and Joyce slept on the floor, but again we were dropped onto Joyce so that she could look after us. Finally, Joyce put her bedding in the whelping box so it smelled of her and our gypsy days were over. Occasionally we were found in odd corners of the room, and to add to the fun, one of my brothers was retrieved from the rubbish sack amongst the dirty newspapers! Ailsa even found time to offload a couple of us by jumping the gate and depositing us with Emma in the downstairs cloakroom! Emma couldn't help out with the feeding as she had been spayed.

When Ailsa's human mum returned, we survived a short car journey to our mum's house. We had larger accommodation as we were growing fast, and during the day, we had a lovely patio and dog kennel to play hide and seek in. A huge Hosta gave us shade, but by the time we left for our new homes, all you could see was the pot!

Kizzy and Emma's Mum came to see us every few days. She didn't come every day as she needed to recuperate from those hectic days, sleepless nights and going to work too! I was eventually chosen to spend my life with Kizzy and Emma and my new name is Muffin. If you have been reading the Dog Diary, you must have known I was destined for disaster. I returned to my birthplace and was introduced to my half-sister Kizzy (we have the same father), and Emma my fawn friend. I soon learned that Kizzy would tolerate me but Emma was going to take her time. I knew I would have to work into her affections gradually.

Guess what? I reacted against my parvovirus jab and nearly died. I just couldn't keep my food down and visited the vet daily. He said he couldn't put me on a drip (whatever that was), he said it was extremely unkind for one so young. My new Mum spent four days and nights feeding me liquid every hour, monitoring my progress. It was suspected at first that I had pyloric stenosis, which is a malfunction of the exit valve to the stomach. A barium X-ray proved negative. The veterinary pharmaceutical company was informed of my reaction to the drug. I started to improve after the chalk had lined my stomach, and with a special diet and lots of love and attention I started to put on weight. No photos were taken of me for a long time as Mum said I looked like an emaciated cat! When I was thirteen weeks old Ailsa, my canine mum, came to stay as her parents went on holiday. I was over the moon as SHE knew how to play with me. Mum, as usual, had her work cut out. I was dry and clean at night, but, as soon as Ailsa joined us, I started to disgrace myself. It took three nights before the penny dropped: Ailsa was regurgitating her food for my midnight feasts. I was banished to the show cage, which in a way I was pleased about as no-one stole my Bonio that we were given at bedtimes.

Mum was very relieved when Ailsa went home as I continually ignored my mistress and wouldn't do anything she asked of me. Before Ailsa left, she showed Emma how to play with me, so now when Emma is in a good mood, we have a rough and tumble. Kizzy is rather staid and prefers to watch us at a distance with no inclination to join in the fun.

I think I am going to like it here.

MUFFIN 5 MONTHS OLD

1993 – THESE ARE A FEW OF OUR FAVOURITE THINGS 'PENNED' BY KIZZY

With the help of Emma and Muffin after consulting them, I am listing below what we love:

- Rolling in horse, fox, hedgehog, and cow dung whilst Mum's back is turned

- Rubbing our heads all around the valances on the bed

- Stealing the face flannels from the bathroom and rolling on them

- Drinking the loo water if the lid is up

- Standing right in front of the television when we are ignored

- Licking the nearest two-legs after a good drink of water (it helps to dry our beards)

- Continually leaving our toys around the house after armfuls have been collected and put back in our box

- Being given new marrow bones to chew and waiting patiently for one of us to swop over

Beardies World

- Sitting quietly with uplifted faces whilst the vegetables are being prepared and receiving a scrummy raw carrot each

- Barking at thunder

- Leaving nose marks on the inside rear window of the car

- Howling at the *Neighbours* theme tune and the signature tune of *BBC News*

- Being played with and cuddled

- And lastly, best of all, being taken for long walks

KIZZY, EMMA AND MUFFIN

1994 – EXTRACT FROM MY DIARY 'PENNED' BY KIZZY

As we are halfway through 1994, I thought I had better put paw to paper. Reading my previous narratives, you must know nothing goes smoothly here for long. Well, what else can you expect when you have a mistress like ours?

EMMA FEELING LETHARGIC ON DARTMOOR

1993 came and went with our Mum being happy in the knowledge that she had qualified our sister Muffin for Crufts. Emma determinedly holds onto life after being diagnosed with Addison's Disease. On one of our walking holidays on Dartmoor, Muffin and I noticed she was quite lethargic and wasn't joining in charging about with us. Mum took her to the vet and after blood tests we were shocked to hear the news. She was put on medication which helps her and when she is well we are all happy, but when she isn't, we all feel miserable with her.

March 1994 arrived and off went Muffin including her canine mum, Ailsa, to Crufts. We watched out of the window as they drove off, relieved that we would now get some peace and quiet with Dad. When Mum and her friends hadn't arrived home by 9.30pm, we thought it strange, but just before 10.00pm they were home. Well, what a story Muffin had for us!

She and Ailsa had performed their best in the ring to no avail. It was Muffin's first time at Crufts and foremost in her mind was the green carpet and the largest crowds she had ever seen. The reason everyone was late was because Mum was taken ill later on that day. She had tummy-ache and as the queues for the ladies' loos were ten miles long, she and other mothers with children pleaded with an official to be allowed to use one of the men's loos. After much argument this was eventually agreed. The 'official' guided the men to the latrines at the back, to spare their blushes, whilst the stalls were commandeered for the females.

Unfortunately, Mum was really ill and she managed to shoot the bolt to her stall before passing out on the floor with her undies around her ankles! A wheelchair was brought in, and with two security guards at the front moving the crowds, the nurse wheeled Mum rapidly away, her head stuck in a sick bowl. Fortunately for us, Mum's friends fed and watered Muffin and Ailsa while Mum was being looked after.

Joyce Ives

They were going to hospitalise her, but Mum, knowing how worried we would all be (including Dad), decided after four and a half hours she would try to make it home. The car was driven right up on the pavement to the front entrance of the NEC and Muffin and Ailsa watched a very pasty-faced mum being helped into the car still hanging on to a sick bowl. There are not many Beardies who can boast that their Mum had passed out in the MEN'S LOO! Still come to think of it, it was Mothers' Day. Needless to say, poor Mum had to go into

Beardies World

hospital for lots of awful tests with the result that she had a hiatus hernia to add to her irritable bowel syndrome.

IT IS RAINING AND WE ARE READY TO GO OUT FOR OUR WALK
AS YOU CAN SEE WE HAVE TO SHARE THE CONSERVATORY
WITH MUM'S PLANTS

In April, Mum was in trouble again. We three were out for a walk with Ailsa, which was uneventful, until, on returning to our house, we spotted Ailsa's Mum across the road and took off with every exuberance to greet her … A visit, again, to the doctor confirmed that Mum had put some ribs out. So because of us she had to visit an osteopath!

The only good thing in April was another walking holiday staying in Peter Tavy, Dartmoor. The weather was kind to us; and also at the end of this month our master and mistress became grandparents. We can't wait for him to grow up so that he can play with us.

In May all three of us were bursting with pride when we came home from the Southern Counties Bearded Collie Club's Spring Frolic. We passed our tests being judged for the

Kennel Club Good Citizen Dog Scheme and each of us had Certificates to put up on the wall. Mum was especially proud of Muffin as she is only a show dog!

Also in May, a phone call sent Mum and Muffin's breeder down to collect one of Muffin's brothers, as his mistress, due to ill health, had decided to return him. Needless to say we all spent a very traumatic six weeks helping to look after him before finding him a suitable home, but that's another story.

July was another month Mum tried to forget. For reasons only known to herself, she went into the woods at the bottom of our garden, without us I might add. She returned and decided to climb back over the fence, taking a short cut. I heard a crash and I rushed to the bottom of the garden to find Mum on the ground with the wheelbarrow on top of her.

I licked her face and ears, reviving her. Emma and Muffin were useless, deciding to stay away, barking furiously. Dad was playing golf. So, hanging on to me she pulled herself up and hobbled back to the house.

Another visit to casualty, not in an ambulance this time, but taken by Dad, who, when returning home, lashed her with his tongue – which was quite unrepeatable. All three of us were really shocked, but thinking about it, we knew it was because he would have to take over the running of the home, plus exercising us.

It's been brilliant! He gets up an hour earlier and we are raced through the woods for an hour and then when he gets home from work he takes us out again. Mind you, we did not even think of looking at a puddle, let alone jumping in it! Mum just languished on the settee all day with her foot strapped up and elevated. She didn't break her ankle, just tore the tendons and ligaments. It has been whispered that it could take up to eight weeks before she is up and running again.

I said to her, "Well, make yourself useful and get my diary up to date." I wonder what the next six months will bring?

1995 – CHRISTMAS COMES BUT ONCE A YEAR 'PENNED' BY KIZZY

Mum and Dad's Christmas wasn't quite what they expected. Their two legged children were elsewhere. Their daughter was in Australia enjoying a belated honeymoon and their son had relatives staying with them.

So it was to be a quiet and relaxing Christmas. Just us three beardies and Nanny and Jack (Nanny's partner) bringing with them our Westie friend, Pippa. We have had up to thirteen people on Christmas Day before. We then found the plans had changed – just slightly. Dad's bachelor, farmer brother, Uncle Bill, was invited. Just one more – no hardship in that was there?

Dad left early on Christmas morning to pick up Uncle Bill, whilst we had a good run in the woods, to be followed by hovering in the kitchen, relishing all the delicious smells and hoping that something – anything – might drop on the floor. We had been brushed and looked delightful in our red satin bows.

Mum went to have a shower and wash her hair, and changed into her best clothes. The doorbell rang, which she answered, hair dripping, thinking it was one of the neighbours. No, it was Jehovah's Witnesses trying to sell the *Watchtower* magazine. Mum smiled sweetly, conveyed Christmas greetings and they left. We were not sure whether the people at the door left quickly because of Mum's wet hair or whether they couldn't hear themselves speak with us trying to rush out to wish them a happy Christmas.

Happy and humming Christmas carols, Mum was now contemplating what colour nail varnish to wear when the telephone rang interrupting her decision. It was Dad. "Slight hiccup," he said. The breeder of Uncle Bill's six month old Border Terrier puppy, Bruce, was unable to look after him, so he would be bringing the puppy dog as well. Dad finished by saying, "Oh, and by the way he will have to be bathed as soon as he arrives as he is extremely dirty and flea-ridden, being a farm dog."

A relaxed and happy Mum became suddenly agitated. Her dirty clothes were thrown back on again and there was a sudden urgency in her step. The baby gate was put up across the back door, a cardboard box was made into a puppy bed and put out in our sleeping quarters. The grooming table was pulled out along with the hairdryer, and preparations were made for the bath. We thought, "Cripes, it can't be us, she's only just brushed us!" We crept into our bean bags, trying not to draw attention to ourselves. Surely she must be demented, shampooing on Christmas Day – she's lost her marbles! Good heavens, now she has flea-sprayed us, what on earth is going on? We were all feeling very edgy.

Uncle Bill arrived with a little brown dog. We watched as Bruce was rapidly swept up by Mum not even allowing us to say hello to him. We could hear a lot of water being splashed about in our bathroom (the garage). It was midday, dinner was scheduled for 1.00pm, but Mum had everything under control as we watched her dry and groom Bruce. We counted our blessings that it wasn't us going through it on the table.

Out on the patio we were finally introduced to this sweet-smelling, flea-less, tail-wagging tornado. Muffin and I decided that he really wasn't our type and left Emma happily playing with him.

Nanny and Jack arrived with Pippa, our Westie friend and Bruce dropped Emma like a stone, favouring a dog more his size. Emma told us she was thankful as by this time she had had quite enough. Mum took this opportunity to rush upstairs to change her clothes – no time to paint her nails now!

The family still managed to sit down to their Christmas dinner on time whilst they watched Pippa and Bruce dismantling Dad's newly seeded lawn, sown after the drought in the summer. Once Bruce had finally stopped playing, he spent time marking his territory around the garden, then proceeded to leap four feet up the patio windows deciding that he would like some Christmas dinner too. Mum continued to fill up her wine glass, trying to carry on a carefree conversation and put out of her mind the constant barking, turning her head away from the lower half of the windows which were grey and streaked with Bruce's paws.

As Mum dished up the Christmas pudding and mince pies, she happened to glance out of the window to see that I was eating up the potato and carrot peelings along with the outer leaves of the Brussel sprouts. I was only trying to tidy up where Bruce had knocked the bucket over! At least I saved her a journey to the compost heap. I thought it would also take her mind off the other mess out there – Bruce had dug out one of the tubs holding Mum's prize Red Riding Hood tulips, breaking off all the shooting tips, and there was soil scattered all over the patio.

There wasn't much mud in the conservatory though, but the look on Mum's face was quite indescribable. I dived into my bean bag with the brown tornado on top of me chewing my ears. Why do puppies always home in on me? Nanny and Jack were not over pleased either to see their pristine white Westie looking like she needed a bath. I could see Mum mentally saying to herself, no chance! Her eyes travelled around our conservatory, silently noting that Bruce had cocked his leg, marking his territory over our bean-bags, plant pots, the grooming table and yes, even over us! We didn't smell so sweet now. Mum, with a stiff upper lip, removed our beautiful red ribbons, dripping with, well, you know what. At least he did us one favour. We didn't want to wear them anyway.

Uncle Bill took the opportunity to spread himself across the whole settee in a gorged, drunken stupor, whilst Mum took us all for a walk to regain her 'hostess with the mostess' composure, saying to herself, "'Tis the season of goodwill to all men and animals." She kept Bruce firmly on his lead. Returning home we readily settled down for our usual snooze, but Bruce had other ideas, continually barking for more games. Uncle Bill slept through it all. That night Bruce was put in the show crate with his bed. Why Mum was so thick not to think of it sooner, I do not know. We had a peaceful night and we all relaxed dreaming of chewing turkey legs.

On Boxing Day morning, from his usual reclining position on the settee, Uncle Bill directed that Bruce should be let off his lead as he would not run away. The name Boxing Day was quite apt as Bruce proceeded to box and attack one of our male Beardie friends who we met on our walk. We stood motionless in amazement, open mouthed as Mum ran round and round trying to catch that brown monster as he weaved and dived and attacked our dear friend Toby. Very red faced, Mum apologised to the owner who asked her politely if she was enjoying her Christmas, and who the unruly terrier belonged to.

Although Uncle Bill had been invited to stay for a week, Dad decided that as Bruce's behaviour was not improving and Uncle Bill had no intention of using any control whatsoever in teaching Bruce any obedience or manners, he would take them back home after tea. Bruce sauntered out the door, looked back and whispered he had had a fantastic couple of days and looked forward to coming again. No way! I think you have cooked your goose, Bruce.

Beardies World

NAUGHTY BRUCE BEING HELD BY UNCLE BILL

Joyce Ives

LOOKING BACK ON 1996 'PENNED' BY KIZZY

Our usual routine was shattered somewhat in March when Mum started to nag Dad about decorating, which needed to be done before their Canadian cousins arrived in May to stay for two weeks. Dad blamed us and said that it wouldn't have needed doing at all if it wasn't for us Beardies. Mum totally ignored his accusations and said the hall and landing was a 'must' as it was eight years since it had seen a paintbrush. Muffin didn't even know what paint or a paintbrush was! Mum, in fact, was quite clever, and the hall, the kitchen and dining room also got decorated. Wow, these people who were coming must be special.

On the arrival of our guests there was a jam packed itinerary to adhere to. This involved Mum rising at 5.30am each morning whilst everyone else snoozed in bed to make sure we didn't lose out on our exercise. She then had to get back in time to serve breakfast.

At the end of our guests' first week we were all booked to go to the Beardie Spectacular, but Emma had one of her many bad turns (due to her Addison's Disease) and we had to cancel it. The following week, the 'two-legs' had booked bed and breakfast in the Lake District for a couple of days, returning via North Wales to show off the UK's spectacular scenery. We were to go to our usual Beardie friend's house to be looked after. Emma though, because she wasn't well enough to be left with us, toured around with the two-legs. She gradually regained her strength and told us on her return that she had even gone up Mount Snowdon on the train, sitting on Mum's lap enjoying the scenery and of course, watching the sheep!

At the end of September we travelled to Alston on the edge of Northumbria to meet up with our usual crowd for our walking holiday. One of our best walks was when we climbed up the side of England's highest waterfall, The Cauldron Snout. It drops by 200ft (60 metres). In Mum's walking book it mentioned that extreme care was needed to negotiate the climb. Our twelve walkers in the party were puffing, pushing, pulling and heaving everyone up the huge boulders, including Emma and me (as I am a veteran). Muffin, of course, hardly needed any help, being a youngster. Once at the top, the consensus of opinion was – glad we did it – a great experience – but never again!

We had a lovely week, and the weather was kind to us. Emma, surprisingly, kept up with us, often ahead of us, but in the evenings she tucked herself up in her quilt or slept across Mum's lap. She told us she was feeling ill again and didn't want to eat.

A week later, when Dad was away for the weekend playing golf, Emma was really ill, lying on Mum's lap all evening between sickness bouts. Mum stayed with her all night. I sat watching her knowing how ill she was. She had been suffering with Addison's Disease for four years. The last I saw of her was being carried out to the car in Mum's arms at 3.30am.

It took Muffin and me nearly four weeks to stop listening out for cars that stopped outside the house in the expectation of her trotting back in to greet us and even longer to stop looking for her when out on our walks.

Muffin took it very badly as she and Emma slept together. I really felt it should have been me, as I'm eleven and Emma was only nine-and-a- half. I, too, haven't been in good health recently, having had three small strokes in the last year. I'm quite deaf and I'm starting to get arthritis in my front legs.

When I depart over the Rainbow Bridge to join Emma, I shall have to get Muffin to take on my diary. What a depressing thought. Will she remember everything we have done and write it down?

Oh yes, just a little postscript before I sign off. Do you remember my Christmas story about Bruce? Well, the latest is he ran away from the farm one evening, legging it up to the next village where a Golden Retriever was in season. Uncle Bill got a telephone call at 2.00am from the owner asking him to collect Bruce. He had got through the cat flap and the owner came down to a commotion in the kitchen to find Bruce and her Goldie in a compromising position!

Must finish off as Mum is getting our dinner ready. I have an extra treat every day – one pineapple ring- as I keep 'picking up', and it is supposed to stop what they call a disgusting habit!

I managed to get Mum to type this up as she was feeling poorly after dislocating her jaw. It happened when laughing at her own stupidity. She told Dad that she was going to the shops to buy some 'UB40'. Everyone knows that's a pop group. What she meant to say was 'WD40'!

WHO WAS TO KNOW

I gave Mum and Dad permission to enter this into my diary:

WHO WAS TO KNOW
We'd love you so.
Bonding our home with a heart of gold.
A fluffy fawn mite giving years of delight.
Loads of fun watching you grow
We even enjoyed many a show.

WHO WAS TO KNOW
The early years with Kizzy you'd play
None of us knowing for a limited stay.
When Muffin arrived you really strived
To give her your heart
Making her happy, doing your part.

WHO WAS TO KNOW
Then all of a sudden you became ill
No more playing, you became quite still.
Oh horror, Addison's was diagnosed
But from this illness you steadfastly rose.
We kept you well with pills and potions
Our love for you still filled the oceans.

Joyce Ives

WHO WAS TO KNOW
Emma dear, we miss you so much
Your wet nose in the mornings
Waking us with a soft touch.
Your pleading eyes to climb up for a cuddle
Then on our laps you'd curl for a snuggle.

WHO WAS TO KNOW
When out walking, Kizzy and Muffin run ahead
Then they stop – looking back – a moment we dread
Waiting and waiting, their paws are like lead.
They, like us, can't accept you're now dead.
Dear sweet Emma now running elsewhere
Through buttercups and daisies, with not even a care.

WHO WAS TO KNOW

1997 – WHO SAID 'PENNED' BY MUFFIN

Kizzy is taking a break from her diary and asked me to put paw to paper, although SHE SAID I should not tell as it's not very flattering to you know who! I'm young, brash, wild and mischievous. In fact I've got all the attributes a Beardie bitch should have – so here goes.

WHO SAID: it's fun being a Beardie? It's okay when HER INDOORS is running on all cylinders. You know what I mean, nice long walks with your friends, squatting where you please, so SHE has to pick up behind you, having a nice roll in some gooey muck (I find fresh foxes very aromatic). So SHE moans a bit, but one touch of the nose and a flash of those big innocent looking eyes and SHE'S all yours again. Even when SHE goes out without you, the same routine brings out the biccies, it never fails. You get washed, brushed, blow dried, teeth and ears cleaned, real five star luxury.

WHO SAID: it's fun being a Beardie? Certainly not when HER INDOORS has to go to HER vet's hospital to have an operation on HER dewclaw (big toe to you), and what with all the arguing that was going on, I don't think SHE was covered by Petplan! HER vet said she would have to rest with HER paw up for weeks and weeks with everything being done for HER – just like a Beardie really.

WHO SAID: don't worry, it won't seem too long? Certainly no friend of mine. It's been sheer hell since SHE went away the other week. It's like trying to get bones from a butcher to try and get HIM INDOORS to behave like SHE did! Before, when SHE was walking us first thing, HE was still in bed (retired, you know). Now HE has to feed and walk us and it's when HE wants, with not a thought for us.

Breakfast is about half an hour late, our toast often gets burnt, our walk is done at a speed the greyhounds down the local track would be proud of.

WAKE UP DAD, WE WANT OUR BREAKFAST

Stopping for a sniff/roll is definitely a NO-NO unless you can do it in motion (a canine joke). SHE used to lift us into the back of the car if we asked HER to – HE just says 'IN' and if we don't, we walk home!

The gentle hand and soothing tones have been replaced by GIANT HAYSTACKS on a bad day. HE doesn't need a hairdryer after our baths, the hot air generated makes a good substitute.

WHO SAID: you should never wish your days away? All I can say is, it's a pity every one of HIS years is not equal to seven, like ours, because HE would be well past HIS walking days at 420. That way we might get someone who understands our needs better.

What do you mean, Kizzy? I can't say that?

Okay so HE has to cook, clean, wash, iron, shop, walk us,

Beardies World

feed us, keep us clean, look after HER INDOORS so SHE gets better quickly. This means what HE'S doing, HE'S doing for us. I did say I was young, brash and wild, and perhaps I should add, a bit hasty in making judgements to that as well. Perhaps I've been spoilt in the past and now I've seen how hard it is to own a Beardie.

WHO SAID… No, I think I'VE SAID enough!

1998 – THE NEWCOMER

Hi there readers, my name is Solei
And I'm pretty sure it's here I'll stay
With these two Beardies who look like my Mum.
If I play my cards right
They should be quite fun.
I cried and cried the first and second night
But my new friends understood my plight.
Once in the dark I went for a wee
And there was this Monster walking in front of me
In the moonlight – I saw it so clear
When I sat still, so did he!
Help, help, I quivered in horror and fear
Oh relief, it's my shadow, silly me.
With my two new sisters I'm sure I'll be busy.
Have you guessed who they are?
Yes, it's Muffin and Kizzy!

SOLEI – pronounced – SO-LAY

Beardies World

TEA TIME WITH JORDAN

A LETTER HOME TO MY BIRTH MOTHER 'SCRAWLED' BY SOLEI 18TH AUGUST 1998

Dear Mummy,

I thought I would give you an update on how I am faring and to make sure that you have not forgotten me already. I can't remember what you look or smell like now and I am sure you wouldn't recognise me. I am such a big girl now and I'm so grown-up that I haven't slept in my crate for nearly two weeks.

I am extremely busy helping my new Mum and Dad harvest the onions which are ripening in the vegetable patch, and ever so proudly carry one or two onions a day into the house.

Last week I was taken to Uncle Bill's 70th birthday party. My crate came too but Mum and Dad found I didn't need it as I was bouncing around meeting everybody. There were lots of little children there and I was in my element lying on the grass being cuddled and stroked. Jordan, Mum and Dad's grandson, took his paddling pool and I had a lovely time standing up in the water, pretending to swim.

Back at home, I thought I would practise swimming in the water bowls, and I don't know why, but Mum was forever mopping up the kitchen. She was a spoil sport; I thought it was wonderful skidding about.

Yesterday Mum, Dad and Jordan took us all to Marlow for a little walk along the river. There were lots of people and masses of children, also a fair with roundabouts. I thought it was a bit boring just having to sit and watch Jordan going

Beardies World

round and round on a motorbike, and couldn't understand why I wasn't allowed to join him. Lots of people came up to stroke me and Kizzy and Muffin and I was surprised to see one dog wearing a yellow jacket walking alongside a wheelchair. Kizzy told me that was a specially trained dog to look after his disabled master.

Mum and Dad have been busy decorating the front porch and when Mum was putting everything back, she didn't notice that I slipped by her and legged it up the stairs. I was a bit desperate and did a big wee in their bedroom which Mum didn't notice until the end of the day. Now she can't get the stain out!

This will be my one and only letter to you and I do hope my sister and two brothers have written letting you know how they are getting on.

Love,
Solei.

SOLEI WITH MUFFIN

Joyce Ives

MY DIARY ENTRY – 1998
'PENNED' BY SOLEI

Kizzy is allowing me to add to her diary. Well, I am still living here at the same house; I still have the same Mum and Dad and Kizzy and Muffin are still my playmates. Apparently Kizzy's entry in 1986 was about her first year as a puppy as she was Mum and Dad's first Beardie. I know she has been keeping the diary going on and off ever since. She is quite a veteran being twelve-and-a-half years old now and I keep forgetting that when I greet her in the morning I must be a little more gentle, because sometimes she falls over! Kizzy now sleeps in the den at night to give her some peace away from me.

I thought I would put paw to paper to give you an idea of my new experiences, and wow! What fun I am having. When I arrived here, Muffin was terrified of me. All I wanted to do was to cuddle up to her as I missed my canine mum so much. Kizzy allowed me to nestle up to her until I bit her tail – I think I ruined what would have been a beautiful friendship.

Apparently, the routine with puppies in this household is to be taken out in a bag so they can socialise and get used to traffic noise, so I was duly popped into a strong bag with the zip pulled up to where my head poked out. What an experience, I was in awe of this new big world and kept quite still. On the third outing, that was it – no more – if they wanted me to go out with them, then it was to be carried in their arms or not at all. I think they will soon find out I'm a bit different to their other Beardies they have had. Now I have had all my vaccinations I am allowed outside walking on the ground.

I have had a wonderful time with this thing called 'socialising'. I went to a nine-year-old's birthday party with lots of little two-legs running around. At first they were frightened of me, but as the minutes passed everyone took turns to cuddle and stroke me. A couple of weeks later I was taken to a 70th birthday party and again I was busy playing with everyone. We have twice been to a residential home for the elderly with lots of people sitting in chairs not moving at all, just sitting there. My presence brightened their day and one lady who hadn't spoken for months surprised everyone by telling us all that she had dogs when she was younger and even said what a gorgeous puppy I was. Another day I was introduced to two German Shepherd puppies who were three weeks older than me and three times my size. Their names were Toffee and D'Arcy. Guess what, they were terrified of me – all I wanted to do was to say hello and make friends.

We had a lovely afternoon at a place called Marlow, walking along the edge of a huge expanse of water where there were lots of little, medium and large house type buildings floating on it. Kizzy and Muffin laughed at me and said they were called boats. On one very splendid boat there were two very aloof-looking Weimaraners watching us and guess what their owners said to our Mum and Dad. "Oh look, primer, undercoat and topcoat." We have never been called that before. Primer was me, undercoat was Kizzy as Mum had clipped her coat back as she was unable to cope with an hour's grooming as she was so old, and Muffin was topcoat as she had beautiful long flowing tresses.

Mum has also taken me to our town a few times and I have got used to going in the lift from the car park and now take no notice of the hissing noise the buses make when they brake. On market days the pet food stall smells really delicious.

Mum and Dad are finding out, to their cost, that I am definitely a different kind of Beardie and have been in trouble quite a few times. What did I do?

- Dug three large holes in Dad's lovely manicured lawn and a massive hole in a flower bed

- Was caught helping myself to a lovely jam doughnut off the table when we had guests

- Dad thought I was happily chewing a bone, then he noticed I had turned my attention to Mum's spectacles. Well, I was missing her because she had gone to bed early saying she was tired. Surely it's not me that tires her out?

- When I think Dad has watched too much sport on the television, I hide the remote. It is great fun watching him going around all my hiding places, playing hunt the gadget. That's far more entertaining, especially when he can't find it. I follow him around with an innocent expression – I am certain he loves me really.

SOLEI AND MUFFIN GUARDING THEIR FAVOURITE BUSH

When I am a lot bigger, Mum and Dad are taking Muffin and me on a walking holiday. Kizzy will not be allowed to come as she cannot manage long walks any more. This will be another new adventure.

By the way, I am called Solei because Mum says I'm her little ray of sunshine, but Dad says he can see clouds on the horizon!

Joyce Ives

KIZZY'S REFLECTIONS

Why oh why do I have to get old?
It is inevitable, so I'm told.
I'm now thirteen and that's quite an age,
Mum says I'm well past that puppy stage.

I feel quite regal watching the others,
Relaxed in my bean bag, snuggled in the covers.
I'm head of the pack, in fact, Queen Bee,
So look out you two if you dive on me!

Whilst Muffin and Solei rush ahead when we walk,
Those terrible two, the rabbits they stalk.
I just amble along with Mum at my leisure
Watching it all gives me so much pleasure.
I see our new puppy, so full of life, She is always causing us such strife.
Did I really run that fast; was I so carefree?
I gaze in amazement and pretend she is me.

My eyesight is blurred, my hearing not good,
And I bump into things when I'm out in the wood.
My nose is okay, but my joints are quite stiff
But when food is about, I'm there in a jiff.

Beardies World

Why oh why do I have to get old?
My time is near, or so I've been told.
I don't feel ready to go just yet,
Can you get HRT from the vet?

Joyce Ives

DEAR KIZZY

Your ditty made me feel so sad
But there are things to make you glad
That you're not human like all of us
(No more running for that bus!)
You don't get wrinkles on your skin
No saggy bum or double chin
No flabby boobs or haggard face
YOUR old age comes with gentle grace.
YOUR dreams are sweet – of puppy days
Not hopes of plastic surgeries!
Enjoy your days, oh Kizzy dear
You'll look the same this time next year
As for me, I won't I fear!

Love from a human auntie

MY 1999 DIARY
'PENNED' BY KIZZY

I thought I should bring you up to date. To refresh your memories, I'm now fourteen years, one of a trio, with Muffin who is eight and Solei, our baby who is now two years old.

We three own an odd couple called Joyce and John. We try to keep them in check and train them in our Beardie ways, but are not always successful in getting them to do what WE want. They act like teenagers sometimes and rebel!

In February, Mum deserted us for four days, she had to fly to Canada to attend a funeral and left us in control of Dad. Luckily our routine was written down for him so we all survived without her.

In March, Crufts Dog Show was upon us and Solei had qualified for the Puppy Class. She was very proud as she got to the final six, but arrived home with the right side of her muzzle very swollen. Despite many visits to the Royal Veterinary College, they diagnosed it as an allergic reaction and it took over three months to settle.

In May, Dad's brother (Uncle Bill to us), a Christmas tree farmer living near Ware in Hertfordshire, fell over backwards cracking his head. He was in hospital for nearly three months, so we had to learn how to be farm dogs. Uncle Bill's dog, Bruce the Border Terrier, had managed to survive to the age of three. Now there's a friend to admire. He totally controls his two-legged charge and does exactly as he pleases. He has even been taken to Court with Uncle Bill – Bruce being charged with unruly behaviour and was bound over to keep the peace, something about him getting into another garden and killing a child's pet rabbit. Our two-legs said he was a bad influence on us, so whilst Uncle Bill was in hospital, a neighbour looked after him.

During our stay at the farm, Muffin, who is always the goody two shoes, blotted her copy book. Mum caught her with her head in the rubbish bin downing an entire plastic roasting bag that had just been taken off the roasted chicken. Dad wouldn't believe Mum. "Muffin has swallowed the roasting bag? Muffin – you sure – Muffin? You're mistaken! It must have been one of the others!" We watched Muffin looking at Dad with her big goo goo eyes, innocence herself, how dare Dad think it was ME?

Well, they phoned Bruce's vet and as it was a Sunday, there was an answerphone. After leaving a message, they then calmly sat down and ate their dinner! Thankfully the vet phoned and we all piled in the car following directions on how to find the veterinary practice. Dad was still insisting that Mum had been mistaken as to who had swallowed the bag. He is so gullible.

At the vets Mum and Dad were told the swiftest and kindest way (and of course the most expensive) was to administer a couple of drops of a special drug in Muffin's eyes and within three minutes, Muffin gave one big heave and out popped the bag complete with the tie still attached to it. The very next day, Dad went out and bought a new rubbish bin with a snap lid.

The rest of our stay on the farm was uneventful, but we did enjoy the countryside and eleven acres to run on. Uncle Bill came home and we moved out and were pleased to get home to catch up with all our old haunts again.

One other story I must put on record about Uncle Bill. He is such a soft, kind man. He had a goat a few years back and it became ill. The vet gave her an injection and Bill was told to take her home and keep her warm. One of his neighbours called by and found Bill lying in bed cuddling the goat under the bed clothes. Well, the vet did say to keep her warm!

All of us, yes me too, were taken on holiday for a week to St. Agnes in Cornwall. Mum had strained her groin and couldn't walk very well, so Dad did all the early morning walks whilst Mum got the breakfast – usually it was the other way round. It didn't take me long to realise that Mum had been left behind, so as soon as I had done 'my pieces', I ground to a halt and Dad would take me back, then he would go off with Muffin and Solei. It was far more interesting watching Mum cooking the breakfast, such delicious mouth-watering smells too. The weather was kind to us, but we found only one beach that allowed dogs on it and it was so difficult to climb down to and much too hard for me; Mum and Dad abandoned trying. We all love a paddle so we were disappointed.

A few weeks later, Mum was very ill – not related to her cooking – and ended up in hospital for two weeks, caused by an allergy to goat's milk. She already had a cow's milk allergy! The household was in turmoil, and not only did Mum lose weight, but Dad did too. At least the weather was good, so we kept clean for him. Dad did drive us to the hospital car park and Mum was allowed to come down in her dressing gown to give us a cuddle. She was really missing us and we were so sad when she turned away from us and walked back into the big grey building. We were ecstatic when she returned home. The rest of the year was fairly boring for us, we sent Mum and Dad off on their own for a two week holiday to give us a welcome rest. We sometimes find it quite a strain in keeping them in check.

December arrived and we spent Christmas Day being pampered at a relative's house, then Boxing Day it was open house here, with over forty people in and out all day which we found a bit tedious until some of the guests offered to take us for a walk. They thought it would be a good idea, a fun thing to do, but Mum wasn't so pleased to get us back covered in mud and her having to clean us wearing her posh frock. There's gratitude for you!

We had a brilliant New Year, it was supposed to be special, something about Millennium celebrations. Our charges decided they would have a dinner party, and also we were looking after an extra three Beardies as their owners were going out celebrating and didn't want to leave them on their own because of the fireworks being let off. Mum got the 'flu' and Dad was about to go down with it, therefore, the dinner party was cancelled, so us six Beardies had our own party.

After seeing in the New Year, which for our two-legs was a bit of a damp squib, it was finally bed time. We knew Mum and Dad wouldn't be happy sleeping on their own with all that noise going on outside, so to keep them from being upset, we all decided they needed our company especially as they were not feeling well. We wouldn't dream of sleeping in their bedroom normally, totally out of bounds to us, but our Beardie guests had to be shown a little luxury, didn't they?

Our Beardie guests insisted on jumping on Mum and Dad's bed – a complete no-no. Well if they did it, why shouldn't we? What a commotion as we were all trying to make ourselves comfortable. I cannot record Mum and Dad's reaction. Hey ho, welcome to the Year 2000!

MILLENNIUM TAILS

Hi this is me again, you know, Kizzy the storyteller. I really feel I ought to enlighten you on last year, as like most years it was pretty unforgettable.

After seeing in the year 2000 with our Beardie friends, we were quite looking forward to the rest of the year. Our owners did too, well, we have certainly been busy.

Mum, we have decided, is a walking disaster. She is always tripping over, not us I might add, but tree roots, her own feet, etc. etc. Now if she had four legs like us there wouldn't be a problem, would there? Solei, Muffin and me were out exercising Mum in the woods, and we, as usual, were well ahead of her, when Muffin realised that Mum wasn't following. Solei and I carried on but she went back and found Mum had fallen down a big hole in the ground which was an overgrown abandoned children's camp. Being early spring, it was still quite slippery and muddy, and poor old Mum couldn't get up the steep sides. Muffin proudly told us later that she stood right at the edge of the hole and Mum got hold of her mane and gave the command 'back' so Muffin backed up to pull her out. We were really impressed.

In May, Dad tore ligaments in his knee, and ended up in hospital having an operation. He should have only stayed overnight, but was there the whole week. Nothing goes smoothly in our household. Mum and her best friend had booked a week away in Devon with Solei and Barbara's dog Annie (only two dogs were allowed to go), and Dad was supposed to look after Muffin and me, but because of his operation, we had to have a holiday with our other Beardie friends.

Solei and Annie had a wonderful time, but Mum, as usual, did her falling over trick, this time tripping and falling backwards into the sea. She had waded into the sea desperately calling to Solei as she had swum out a long way trying to chase a seagull. Mum was flapping her arms about shrieking to Solei to get her attention. Thankfully Solei abandoned her mission and returned to find Mum with a wet bottom. We had a two mile trip to the nearest pub before Mum could strip off, drying her knickers and trousers under the hand dryer in the ladies' loo!

In June, four of our Beardie friends who lived near Oxford invited us to a barbeque, including another two Beardie guests with their two- legs. The previous day, Mum had bathed me as I had rolled in liquid horse manure, so although I have a short coat, I felt I looked the bees' knees – white where I was supposed to be white. The nine of us had a wonderful time, especially as one of them was a boy! We all enjoyed exploring the huge garden; it was quite a warm sunny day, so I decided to take a dip and swam with the goldfish, much to the displeasure of Mum and Dad. When trying to get out I sank all the beautiful water plants and churned up the mud. Mind you, I wasn't the only one to behave badly. The Beardie boy, I will not mention his name, but you know who you are, kept climbing on the table to steal the food. When it started to cloud over and the two-legs were feeling chilly, the tables were cleared to take everything back inside.

Mum was carefully carrying a plate of chocolate biscuits and the Beardie boy, yes you again, deliberately flipped his muzzle under Mum's hand and shot the plate of biscuits up into the air onto the floor. Such skill. He had obviously been practising. Of course all nine of us demolished the lot; our owners couldn't eat them, could they? We had a lovely day, especially as we were all given marrow bones to chew.

In August, Dad's eldest brother, Uncle Bill the farmer, was very ill and was in hospital for three weeks, so once again we were down on the farm pretending to be farm dogs. Bruce, his naughty Border Terrier was looked after by a neighbour in the village again, giving us a fairly quiet time. There were no fences to keep Bruce in – he had never been trained so was always running off.

Mum and Dad were kept busy looking after one hundred and fifty potted tomato plants and two hundred runner bean plants. It made us snigger a bit as Mum had only four tomato plants and twenty runners back at home. The five thousand Christmas trees had to be looked after too. We helped by chasing the deer off as they kept nibbling the new shoots on the younger trees.

At the beginning of October, Mum and Dad took us all on holiday to a lovely place called Winfrith Newburgh in Dorset. Absolutely fabulous walking country and it wasn't at all muddy.

One of the days, we went to Swanage to a steam railway station, a new experience for all of us. This huge, big, puffing engine pulled in and Solei was terrified when the driver released the steam pressure. It hurt our ears, nothing like bus air brakes at all. She shook for the first few minutes of the journey, but then decided it wasn't so bad after all so we happily watched the passing countryside. At Harman's Cross, we got out, and as it was lunchtime, we crammed into the tiny waiting room and ate our lunch which helped to make Dad's backpack lighter.

With Dad following a map, we made our way back to Swanage. We had a lovely time, so many exciting smells, walking through grassy fields and into woods, then it was spoilt by two newly ploughed fields which we found almost impassable. We then had a fair bit of road walking to do, being so old, I lagged behind. At this point Mum and Dad were also questioning whether they too were not cut out for walking holidays. For goodness sake, they are nowhere near as old as me!

Our holiday accommodation was rather cramped, but we soon found our own little niches, though were often woken at night to hear the bed squeaking. No, it's not what you are thinking: Dad was using the bed as a trampoline to bang on the ceiling as there seemed to be an infestation of mice holding a clog dance in the loft.

On another day, Mum experienced a bit of excitement. We spent a day exploring Studland Bay following the nature trails. This we all enjoyed, walking along the sandy beach. It was cold, but quite sunny and we were really having a wonderful time. I, as usual, was lagging behind and noticed a man sunbathing amongst the sand dunes. Well, if I see someone at floor level, I have to go and investigate and say hello. We Beardies are so friendly, don't you agree? I increased my step towards him. Mum and Dad were ahead with Muffin and Solei, great! I had him all to myself without the others butting in!

He must have been asleep because he jumped up shouting as I licked a happy greeting, although I didn't care much for the taste of suntan oil. Mum came running across quite red in the face, not embarrassed because I had disturbed him, but because the section we were walking through was a nudist beach and this man looked ready to have a bath.

Mum apologised for me waking him, making only eye-to-eye contact. As we hurriedly walked away, with me firmly clipped on my lead, lots of heads suddenly popped up at various points in the sand dunes and they were ready for their baths too! Making our way back to the car Mum just wouldn't stop giggling. She said it was the icing on the cake – the end of a perfect day!

Although we enjoyed our holiday, we were pleased to go home and it was just as well because the weather changed, starting to rain.

At the end of October, we were quite shocked to find that Muffin had a chronic heart condition. Her heart is huge and still growing, and she has to take medication twice a day. She knows exactly what time she has to have it, so if Mum forgets, Muffin gives her a nudge. The vet said Muffin only had a while to live. She is only eight and as I am fourteen poor Solei may soon be on her own, maybe Mum will change her name to Solo.

AUTUMN TIME – 2000

It's me, Kizzy, again. As I'm not doing much nowadays, Mum prompted me to continue with my diary entries.

I'm feeling really really ancient and in an effort to keep my old mind ticking over I'm trying to recollect things I haven't previously recorded.

I remember once when I was four years old and Mum was walking Emma and me in the woods. (Emma sadly crossed over the Rainbow Bridge five years ago, aged nine.) We were playing our usual hide and seek game. Emma used to hide behind trees and pounce out at me, but I always knew she was there, because either her tail or her nose was showing! If we went too far from Mum she used to call us and Emma, being the youngest, was the first to return.

On this particular day, unbeknownst to Emma or Mum, I had dashed down a bank to hide from Emma, saw a rabbit, chased it and had got caught up in a thicket of blackberry brambles. The rabbit popped down a hole, but oh dear, I was stuck fast. I could hear Mum's voice beginning to change into a very loud forceful shout calling me, but me being a wimp, I just stayed quiet. Her voice got fainter including Emma's barking. I couldn't understand why Emma hadn't tracked me and shown Mum where I was. Apparently they went back to the car thinking I was there, but of course I was nowhere to be seen.

I stood trembling. Had they abandoned me? No, I could hear them again; Mum commanding Emma to 'find Kizzy'. I couldn't see them, but knew they would find me so didn't think it necessary to bark my happiness at hearing them again.

Emma was hopelessly dancing around, not being helpful at all. Mum thought the logical way was to zigzag across the woods near to where she had seen me last. To me, it seemed an absolute age trying to tear myself free, my long coat making the brambles hold me even tighter.

Mum eventually spotted me. Boy, was I glad to see them both. She spent over ten minutes trying to untangle my fur from the brambles to release me. I was extremely grateful and kissed Mum's face and her bleeding fingers which were full of painful thorns. It had taken an hour to find me, an adventure not to be repeated.

Back to the present time. I'm lying in my bean bag watching Mum prepare the lunch. Muffin and Solei are outside and the door is closed. Mum is always fascinated as to how they know when she is peeling carrots. She can peel potatoes and everything is quiet, then she starts on the carrots and there is an immediate thumping on the back door and in they come waiting for their carrot titbit.

She is silly not knowing why. I know. It's because peeling potatoes is quieter with short strokes, but carrots are a rougher texture and it makes a longer harsher sound. Sometimes Mum turns the radio up loud to try to confuse them, but if indoors we can of course smell them. I can't be bothered getting out of my bean bag because I know I will be handed my share. No, I'm not spoilt, I'm almost fifteen and it is my right to expect first class service at my age!

In the mornings, Mum creeps by me, stopping a while to check I'm still breathing. I know she's there, but keep my eyes tight shut and try to hold my breath, but eventually give in. Then she moves on to take Muffin and Solei out for their run. 7.00am is way too early for me, I get an extra hour in bed before I'm served my breakfast.

Once Mum has also eaten, I look up at her expectantly knowing she will then take me out on my own, which is wonderful because I can walk at my own pace. I'm a bit stiff in the mornings and only manage 200 yards, but in the afternoon I walk with the others and happily slowly walk a mile. Everywhere is closed off, no woodland walking as there is a foot-and-mouth epidemic. It is really boring though, as we are pavement walked or only have two parks to exercise in. There are so many bouncy dogs about, I do get a bit worried sometimes trying to avoid being knocked over. We mustn't complain, at least we can't catch foot-and-mouth.

Yawn, I'm really too tired to write any more, another day perhaps.

EPILOGUE

Kizzy had cancer and to save her suffering, she went to sleep on the 24th June 2001, just six days after her sixteenth birthday.

She had been such a good friend, full of joy and love which she gave freely to all who came in contact with her.

Our first Beardie and leader of our pack, she is greatly missed, and never forgotten.

Rest in Peace dear Kizzy, say hello to Emma for us.

Joyce, John, Muffin and Solei

Joyce Ives

KIZZY IN HER YOUNGER DAYS

KIZZY WRITING HER DIARY

TIME HEALS AND WE BOUNCE BACK 2002

It is almost two years since we lost the leader of our pack, Kizzy. My name is Muffin and I am eleven years old, and my best buddy is Solei who is five. We own an oldish couple called Joyce and John – Mum and Dad to us – and we think we keep them in pretty good order. Life with them is hardly ever boring as we never seem to have a week that runs smoothly.

The beginning of last year is a bit blurred, but we had a lovely weekend away staying with our Beardie friends whilst Mum and Dad stayed at Bourton-on-the-Water for their fortieth wedding anniversary. The hotel did welcome dogs but we thought we would send them there alone!

We were just settling back at home when we packed our bean bags again to stay at our Uncle Bill's, who is the local Christmas tree farmer at Dane End in Hertfordshire. He was in hospital for six weeks, so we looked after Bruce – his naughty Border Terrier – who at seven years old is still a nightmare, as he was always running off to the village. We spent the majority of our time keeping the deer away as they love nibbling the new shoots on the Christmas trees, making them harder to sell, being misshapen. Once home again, we settled into our normal routine and enjoyed catching up with our friends and checking out all the new scents in our happy hunting grounds.

Oh yes, then we had another bereavement. Mum and Dad looked after Charlie the Hamster for their eldest grandson

Jordan. We loved him coming to stay; Solei often rubbed noses with him through the bars of his cage. He suddenly went down with an illness called 'wet tail' and Mum had to take him to our vets. He had an injection to try to make him better, but sadly he died five days later. We witnessed the burial sitting quietly whilst Mum, after digging a small hole in Jordan's garden buried his tiny coffin placing flowers and a tiny cross. Jordan was very sad when he came home from holiday. He has a new hamster now called Sammy, but we haven't been asked to look after him. Surely it wasn't our fault that Charlie died?

During August, Mum and Dad's other two grandsons came to stay with us for four days. We love them coming because they play with us. Of course we sat quietly under the dining table during meal times, and it was definitely to our advantage as Lewis aged three, and Connor, aged four, never seemed accurate in finding their mouths. We never have that trouble! Unfortunately, they were very ill with cryptosporidium, and Mum and Dad caught it too, but not us, thank goodness. They couldn't go home as their Mum and Dad had won a holiday in Paris. It should have been such a happy time, but we were totally exhausted with their unhappy crying, so instead of having cuddles we kept out of their way.

MUFFIN, LEWIS AND CONNOR BEFORE THEY WERE ILL

Now on a brighter note, we really enjoyed the 'Tramps Tuck-In' last September. The baked bean juice was absolutely delicious. There was a new trophy to be won called 'The Kizzy Trophy'. The game to be played was called 'Kizzy Says', like 'Simon Says'. Our Beardie friends that played it were so clever, Solei and I were really impressed and Kizzy over the Rainbow Bridge must have been really proud.

We had a lovely day playing with all our friends and once home settled down to a good sleep, but being forever watchful, you know, one eye open, one eye closed, ears always cocked, we realised that Mum was packing again. Dad was off on a golfing holiday to Dorset and we were off to the Christmas tree farm to keep Uncle Bill company for four days.

We spent some time taking Uncle Bill to visit relatives which was a bit boring, although we did get quite a few admiring looks from people on our travels. You know what we mean, when a car follows our car, or overtakes and you see all the smiling two-legs looking at you, it really makes you feel special doesn't it? Yes, and we know it, don't we?

During one of our walks, when Uncle Bill had his afternoon nap, we were cutting through the valley between two fields making our way back to the farm when we spotted another farmer on his tractor making his way down the field to us. Mum thought she had met him down the local pub when we took Uncle Bill for a pint the night before, so she greeted him happily expecting to pass the time of day with him. No, she was wrong and was told the valley track was not a footpath and please remove ourselves forthwith. After explaining she was the sister-in-law of Uncle Bill at Highview Farm (everyone in the area knows him) and just taking a short cut, we saw the farmer frowning at Bruce and in a threatening voice said, "If my wife finds that dog in her kitchen once more, I'll call the police!"

Mum confirmed she would relay his message to Uncle Bill, then we rapidly walked on and if Mum had a tail, hers would have been between her legs. All Uncle Bill said when we returned home was: "I can't understand how people are so intolerant these days, that track used to be a bridle path years ago."

SOLEI HOPING TO DRIVE UNCLE BILL'S TRACTOR

At the end of September, we had a week's walking holiday at Markbeech in Kent with Mum and Dad's two-legged friends. Six humans and us, including our best friend Annie who is an elderly brown whippet/German shepherd dog, but whippet size. We stayed in a 14th century farmhouse, the oldest in the village, and our sleeping quarters was a children's playroom. The house was massive, oak beams and lots and lots of spiders' webs; the spiders had long delicate legs and tiny bodies. Every time Mum had a bath after a long day's walking, the baby spiders plopped into her bath water – the steam must have made them lose their footing.

The farmhouse was built on a hillside so practically every room downstairs and upstairs had a step up or down. We had two huge tiled steps to go down into the kitchen, which were very smooth and worn into a hollow. I had extreme difficulty in getting up them and slipped, hurting my hip. I was so thankful for Mum's massage and for her giving me the confidence helping me every time I needed to go up them. Even one of the two-legs slipped down them, hurting her bottom.

The weather whilst we were there was lovely and hot. We walked some of the footpaths through exciting countryside with wonderful smells; six miles was easy-peasy for Solei, but I was a bit tired, so to be kind to me, we did a smaller walk the following day.

Another lovely walk we did was in the Ashdown Forest. Dad stopped every so often to check the Ordnance Survey map and was told by other walkers that even the army have been known to lose themselves. We were all weary after walking seven miles, but had a break waiting for Annie to return after tracking a deer. We could hear her yipping a good mile away. When she finally arrived back, much to everyone's relief, her Dad said: "Roll up that tongue of yours and put it away!"

We spent practically every lunchtime at a dog-friendly pub, but Annie again was in trouble as she sneaked around the bar into the kitchen to the rage of the Chef who toed her backside out of the door yelling, "Get that dog out of my kitchen!" Our fat brown friend is always greedy, she never waits like us – Solei and me are always given a few chips when we get back in the car.

ANNIE

Our week's holiday whizzed by and we couldn't believe the cars were being loaded again which included local wine and bottles of cider. Everywhere we had visited, we heard tales of woe from the locals telling us that the foot-and-mouth problem was still killing their businesses, as the tourists still hadn't returned.

Once home, we were especially spruced up to visit a very unhappy boy Beardie called Paddy; he had just been re-homed for the second time and we played with him for a while to help him to feel less anxious. His coat was quite short as he had to have an anaesthetic so his vet could groom him and cut the knots out, and he was also very thin. We are glad to hear from Mum each time she visits him that he has settled in with his new owners and they adore him. He is going to be taken to all the Beardie functions to be socialised.

Unfortunately, we didn't go to the Spring Frolic this year as Mum and Dad had booked a walking holiday near Trellech, Monmouth, not realising that the dates clashed! Shame on them!

OH DEAR!

LIFE IN RETIREMENT
2003

It is well over a year since I put paw to paper. I am now twelve years old, and, if you remember, I have an enlarged heart which was diagnosed four years ago and Mum and Dad was told I only had 'a while' to live. Well, I am proving my vet wrong, marvellous this modern medicine nowadays. Solei is now six and we make a great team.

As I mentioned, we enjoyed a week in Trelleck last May. The owners of the 17th century property we stayed in were most impressed with our good manners and we soon settled in, finding niches with interesting smells. I sat upon the landing, leaning against a very large book case whilst having a senior moment, watching the suitcases being brought up. To my great surprise, the middle shelf of the books gave way and I fell into a secret bedroom. How was I to know it was a door?

The day we should have been at the Spring Frolic, we went to a very pretty place called Beacon Hill. We climbed up 365 steps – no, we didn't count them, it was written on a notice board. Over three quarters of the way up, we came to a metal open stairway and Solei and I were terrified as we could see through them to the ground hundreds of feet below. We refused to follow Mum and Dad even though they disappeared from our sight, calling us; we gave each other that knowing look and sat waiting for them to come back. It had taken us quite a long while to climb that far and Mum and

Dad were determined we were to follow them. Well, our initial happiness at seeing them again was short-lived as we had our leads clipped on and were both helped, trembling up the noisy metal steps to the top, being told not to look down. We would rather have been at the Spring Frolic! The confidence in our guardians was really challenged for the first time in our lives and we were extremely grateful to reach the top safely. We raced away from the horrible stairway, looking back at it, praying that we didn't have to return the way we came. Further on there was a most beautiful view at the Windcliffe Vantage Point where we could see an eagle's nest which overlooked the River Wye, plus the old and new road bridges crossing the River Severn in the distance. We were relieved that Mum and Dad found another way down.

Another lovely day was spent at Symonds Yat; first of all making our way up to where lots of twitchers were watching through binoculars at peregrine falcons nesting in the rocky cliffs. We were in our element with all the attention we received from the friendly holidaymakers. Later on we walked down to the river and had a pub lunch, meeting more friendly people.

Later, we were asked to jump into a hand-operated ferry boat to cross the river. We knew we had to sit still as neither of us like deep water, nor does Dad. On reaching the other side there was a very long walk beside the river, so many new and exciting smells, so much to explore. It seemed ages before we again crossed the river over a very high narrow bridge and walked all the way back to our dog mobile where we threw ourselves in the back, exhausted. Mum and Dad sat in their armchairs on wheels to transport us back to our accommodation. Another day was spent trekking through the Brecon Beacons to visit friends whose garden was literally cut out of the mountain side – very pretty but extremely hard work to maintain; we didn't even attempt to climb around it. Our last day was spent walking the Sculpture Trail, which we all enjoyed tremendously.

ON THE FERRY BOAT

Home again, back to the usual routine, catching up with our canine friends and spending a busy time over at Uncle Bill's farm in Hertfordshire. The deer must have 'got wind' of us coming, as we couldn't find any amongst the trees.

The weeks passed by and once again Mum and Dad were packing. Oh great, another holiday. Boxes were in every room and the suitcases were out. It was certainly taking a long time getting ready for this holiday; it must be a really long one considering all we were taking.

Solei and I looked at one another as Mum put us in the dog mobile and we were driven to our little brown friend Annie's house and left there. What was going on?

After lunch, we were walked by Annie's guardians, Auntie Barbara and Uncle Michael, and then driven to another village, stopping outside a bungalow just as two great lorries were leaving.

We trotted in, saying a quick hello to Mum and Dad and sniffed around. So this is our holiday home – not bad, but boxes everywhere, we will have to complain to the owners. Fancy renting this, it was so untidy. We squeezed by all the cartons and found ourselves in the garden; it was like a jungle, lots and lots of little paths winding in and out of trees, shrubs and flower beds. This was brilliant, we could easily hide out of view! Mum and Dad could keep the untidy indoors, we knew this holiday was going to be great. Our stomachs eventually brought us back inside again and we were surprised to see our sleeping cots – usually we only take our duvets. (Mum had dumped our bean bags as they took up too much room.) Evening came and things were quite chaotic; the council had been to exterminate a wasps' nest, and, because of the fumes, we were not allowed to sleep in the conservatory. That night, after lights out, we were able to use the open plan dining room, kitchen and lounge and, as usual, we wandered about, familiarising ourselves with the layout of our new holiday home. Oh, the lounge seemed very familiar; they had even brought the settee and armchairs with them.

Next morning we were awoken to, "Excuse me, what's this I see?" Mum, hands on hips was staring at us. I was full length on the settee, my head comfortably resting on the arm and Solei was curled up in one of the armchairs. Let's face it, everything in this property smelt alien, but as they were so kind to bring our suite (even though we are not allowed on it normally) we thought we would put it to good use. It was good while it lasted.

Weeks and months had gone by, and it suddenly dawned on us that this was not a holiday. This was our new home, they must have moved for me as they knew it was a struggle to climb the stairs in the old house. This can't be Mum and Dad's retirement bungalow; they haven't stopped working since the day we moved!

Mid-June we were off to Knole in Somerset for a week's break as Mum and Dad decided – or should I say Mum decided – that we all needed a holiday, as they had been working very hard decorating and gardening. I will let you know how it goes.

P.S. Solei here. I took Mum to the Spring Frolic in May. We left Dad and Muffin behind, as Muffin wasn't too well. The weather was great and the venue was packed with cars carrying all my friends, I soon singled out the boys and flirted my white socks off.

I was very proud at winning a rosette for the musical chairs event; I didn't really enjoy the game going around the chairs, a bit boring really, BUT, one Beardie Boy had a great time chatting up one of the Beardie Girls he was following, he liked her perfume so much that she had to be moved up the line! What a great day out; where else could you go, having all that delicious food and entertainment for £5.00?

BEARDIE PATROL

I hide in the bushes, watching, waiting,
Eyes open, watching, waiting.
Here it comes along the fence
Plumed tail twitching.
It doesn't see me, I lay so still.
Oh, oh, it's about to leap on the table,
I make my move and in I rush,
It's so quick it's gone in a flash.
So once again I'll be waiting.
The squirrel's here – I really hate him
He eats the seed that's for our friends
They rely on me to make amends.
I seek him here, I seek him there,
But never mind, I won't despair.
One day … Just one day …
After all I am Solei!

Beardies World

ONE DAY – ONE DAY I WILL CATCH YOU

Joyce Ives

OUR 2004 HOLIDAYS

Another year has passed and Solei and I are the luckiest Beardies living in Tylers Green.

We always expect one holiday, so we couldn't believe being taken on another one; we must have been very good girls. Mid-June, we travelled from Buckinghamshire to a beautiful hamlet called Knole in Somerset on a warm and sunny day. Our cosy cottage was called The Old Haybarn. We didn't have any hay to lie on but as soon as our quilts were put down, we dived on them and watched with great interest as everything was unpacked, especially noting where our stash of food was put. Once Mum and Dad were satisfied everything was in the right place, we were thrilled to be taken for a walk around Knole, talking to the very friendly locals, who told us where the dog-friendly pubs were … most important, in fact, a priority! Well bless our white paws, we were met with a very strange sight indeed: practically every cottage had a motionless figure in its front garden. A lady sitting asleep beside a small table with a glass in her hand; some funny man dressed as a footballer; a man with a yellow helmet on up a ladder strapped to a GPO post; a little girl in a pretty dress resting on a big hoop and many, many more. We found out later that there was a scarecrow competition. Mum thought it would be good to enter Solei as she always has bits of twigs, brambles and straw sticking out of her coat!

We awoke to a cloudy day on Sunday and walked alongside the river Yeo at Little Load. To our surprise a heron snapped up an eel from the river and devoured it in less than a minute, quicker than us eating our dinner. We didn't walk too far as the footpath was grossly overgrown and impassable. Remembering the heron, we walked back hoping to see it again, but no luck. We did find a pub garden to lie in as dogs were not allowed inside. The sun was shining and we were all seated snugly under the sun brolly and savouring the delicious smells from our oldies' dinners, when suddenly it started to pour with rain. Anyone seeing us finish our meals sheltering under a sun brolly must have thought we were mad. We didn't have far to leg it to our dogmobile and returned to our cottage.

Monday dawned hot and sunny; the knapsacks were filled with lunches (Bonios for us) and we drove to Burnham on Sea. We spoke to a poodle called Mitzi, who told us, in her posh French accent, that we were only allowed to walk around the yachting basin. She advised us to travel a bit further to Uphill where we could actually drive onto the sands to have our picnic. Arriving there, we eagerly looked around as Dad drove towards the beach, but he decided the sand at the entrance looked too soft, so we had to park in the road and walk to the beach.

Just as we were deciding where to sit for lunch, two cars shot by us, racing along the sands, so Dad went back to get our dogmobile, as the weather looked unsettled and at least if it rained we could have our picnic in the dry. Well, we waited and we waited, and finally we started to walk back as Mum was getting worried. We turned the corner to find Dad on his hands and knees trying to dig our transportation out of the sand. Mum dumped the knapsacks and went to help, whilst we amused ourselves by chasing the seagulls. An hour later the car was free, with extra help from a friendly local and Dad again parked it back on the road. As we settled down to eat our picnic another car got stuck. Our picnic was abandoned for another two hours. The owner of the car said she drove down onto the sands every day to exercise her spaniel and had never been stuck before, so Dad didn't feel so silly it happening to him. We walked further down the beach, well out of sight of any other cars to finish our picnic, but we had to leave immediately afterwards as the sun had come out again, so there was no shade for us. Mum and Dad were not particularly pleased with our jaunt to the sea and they drove home in silence. We couldn't believe that not one sandcastle was built, especially considering the amount of sand they moved!

Tuesday was a much better day as we walked around Ham Hill Country Park meeting a lovely rescue German shepherd dog; he told us he was very happy living with his new owner. We stood and watched the wardens cutting and bagging the ragwort flowers to stop them seeding, telling us they would return later to dig up the roots when they had more time. Not sure whether everyone knows it is extremely poisonous. From the park we walked through the woods and climbed up to St. Michael's Hill. Mum and Dad took it in turn to climb the tower. They wouldn't allow us up there to see the view, as the circular stone stairs were too narrow for us. Back at the country park we had our lunch at a recommend dog-friendly pub. As the day had cooled down we drove to East Lambrook Manor and were pleased to have a sleep whilst the oldies walked around the gardens. They – no, sorry, Mum – bought six specialist plants, most surprising as our garden back at home is jam-packed with trees, flowers and shrubs. Well, that is what we heard Dad say under his breath.

Wednesday was a most relaxing day, as we had gale force winds and rain, so apart from our short comfort walks, we lay resting whilst Mum and Dad read books and watched television. Thursday was a lovely, hot and sunny day, and we spent two-and-a-half hours walking on leads around Hestercombe House gardens. We were fascinated seeing the waterfall, lake and ornamental gardens. Mum took lots of photos there. Lunch was spent hidden under the table in the shade. On the way back to our cottage Mum and Dad stopped at the Willow and Wetlands Centre, and we rested in the shade whilst they looked around. Dad was pleased, as they only looked this time and his wallet stayed in his pocket.

The owner of our cottage suggested that we spent our last day walking around the National Trust gardens at Stourhead, as he assured us dogs were allowed. We drove into the beautifully kept impressive grounds and were alert with anticipation of our day ahead. WRONG – NO DOGS – only in the winter. They ought to rename it NATIONAL DON'T TRUST DOGS. Mum decided that to leave us for an hour parked under the trees in the shade was a definite NO-NO; apart from the hot weather, Mum was worried we might be stolen. Instead, we drove to a restaurant for lunch and there we were allowed in the garden, keeping cool under a sun brolly.

We enjoyed our week's break, but were disappointed with the overgrown footpaths and lack of signs. Although a beautiful area, it was not a good choice for country walking.

July and August were very busy months. Mum and Dad reorganised some of the flower beds, digging out dead trees and shrubs and moving stuff about. We loved this because as they cleared a section, it was dug up and horse manure and compost was introduced, making it lovely and soft and smelly for us to walk over, roll in or dig a hole to lie in. They were not best pleased when we brought the garden indoors on our coats and paws.

Mid-September arrived and we were packing again for a week's holiday at Brompton Ralph in Somerset. Another lovely, cosy cottage, some of it dated back to the 15th century. A Rayburn in the kitchen kept the downstairs beautifully warm. Our two-legs have picked a better area this time.

The morning after our arrival, we travelled to Tarr Steps, crossing the river over a 500-year old bridge of huge stones. We walked three miles over fields and through woods and then back over the stones again. A short walk away we managed to get a table at the inn there, just as it started to pour with rain. Every table had a dog under it and as Mum and Dad ate their scrumptious smelling meal, we noted some other humans' bad manners in that they were feeding their pets from the table. Next, we travelled to a pretty village called Exford, and then on to Dunkery Beacon; the climb was worth the fabulous views.

CROSSING TARR STEPS

Beardies World

On Monday we drove through the Exmoor National Park to Lynmouth, the scene of the 1958 disastrous flood. The high water mark has to be seen to be believed at Lyn Gorge. I didn't really enjoy walking up the Gorge, as it was hard work for me. Solei, however, had no trouble at all as she is half my age! Later, we played on the beach for a while and I watched Solei tossing the seaweed up in the air then rolling on it. She was so happy, it was the sort of thing I did when I was younger. Lunch was pleasant, we passed the time of day with Bertie the Basset Hound who was with his guardians at another table. We were rewarded later with mini ice cream cones: delicious. Returning to our cottage, we called in at Selworthy National Trust Village (dogs allowed on leads), passed through Minehead and checked out Blue Anchor Bay (dogs allowed).

Tuesday, we awoke to torrential rain which flooded our back porch. We went to Minehead again to visit one of Nanny's old war friends who was aged 90. Whilst they were reminiscing, we took the opportunity to have a sleep. Wednesday we drove to Combe Sydenham Country Park. We had a one-and-a-half mile hard climb to the viewpoint. There was a beautiful view of the sea in the distance, but we dogs didn't enjoy it because we had to be kept on our leads, as the place was a breeding area for pheasants. Mum and Dad were not impressed and do not recommend visiting there. However, the day improved as we stopped at Monksilver and had a pub lunch in the beautifully kept gardens. Dad asked the landlord if dogs were allowed inside if it had been raining and the answer was yes. Mum had boar and venison pie; it smelt so yummy but unfortunately she ate it all. We were told that Catworthy Reservoir had very pretty walks, so on Thursday we drove there. NO DOGS! We travelled instead to Wimbleball Lake, which was great for us. Loads of walks to choose from, between three and nine miles. Naturally, because of me, we chose the three miler.

The old town of Dunster is worth a visit. We had lunch in a very pretty courtyard and again practically every table had a dog beside it. When the waitress saw that we were not fed from the table, when bringing the bill, she asked if we would accept a biscuit each for being so good. Now that is what we call dog friendly. We left there to look at the ancient Packhorse Bridge where Solei enjoyed a paddle – I'm too old for such childish pranks. Returning through the town, we were stopped by the antique shop's owners, who gave us kisses and cuddles. They had just lost their Beardie to old age and were awaiting a new puppy from an expected litter. We hope they chose well.

On Friday morning, our last day, I wasn't feeling too well. It was also raining, so we all settled down to watch television for a couple of hours whilst I slept. Having the rest, I started to feel better; the rain had stopped so we drove to Willington. Solei and I rested in the dogmobile whilst Mum and Dad visited the Bakelite Museum. If any of you two-legs are in the area, it is definitely worth a visit as it will bring back so many memories for your older humans. Mum and Dad couldn't stop talking about it on the way to Watchet where we were allowed in a dog-friendly café. The beach at Watchet was full of boulders and I had difficulty in negotiating my way, so we didn't stay long, and, besides, we had to drive back to our cottage to pack up for our return journey.

There has been talk that Mum and Dad are taking an aeroplane to their holiday destination in 2005. Although canines can now get passports to go abroad, I am not well enough to travel. We are sure we will get a break later in the year; they wouldn't dare not take us away at least once a year.

Beardies World

DECEMBER 2004 to SEPTEMBER 2005

A week before Christmas, Mum took us to join Dad on Uncle Bill's Christmas tree farm. He had been there for three weeks helping his other brother Ken to get organised for the rush. Dad was very pleased to see us, especially Mum, as he knew he wouldn't have to get his own breakfast and cook his dinner after work. We soon settled into the new routine and enjoyed meeting all the people wandering around the farm choosing a tree and having it dug for them knowing it was nice and fresh.

Before we arrived we missed some excitement when the local hunt rode right over Uncle Bill's land with their deerhounds. (That's supposed to be our job, keeping the deer away.) The Ives brothers were furious telling the 'whipper in' to get the horses and dogs off the land. Our customers could have been hurt in the stampede. They apologised and left!

Mum and Dad suggested that Uncle Bill would like to host a pre-Christmas dinner and he thought it was a good idea. Uncle Bill is an elderly bachelor and his kitchen equipment is rather sparse. When we arrived, the dogmobile was tightly packed with all the food and utensils Mum needed. The invitations started at five people, but when word went around the family, it increased to thirteen to sit down with a further three people arriving later.

Mum looked quite anxious at times, especially as Uncle Bill's Tricity Viscount cooker is forty-three years old! The relatives arrived including a Dobermann puppy called Simpson, belonging to Mum and Dad's son Duncan. Bruce the Border Terrier took one lunge at Simpson and hung off the end of his ears. Bruce takes an aversion to strange dogs in his home. The mop had to be brought out as poor Simpson peed on the kitchen floor in fright. Bruce was so angry that he then started telling us off as well. That was the end of our dinner party; Solei and I were put in Mum and Dad's bedroom for the rest of the evening and Bruce was shut in Bill's bedroom. What an imposition. Simpson then had the run of the rest of the bungalow, including smelling the delicious turkey and trimmings. Uncle Bill's homemade wine was opened up to find it was off, so while a replacement wine was being fetched from the local shop, the roast potatoes crisped up nicely, saving face for Mum. Uncle Bill managed the soup and main course, but was asleep at the table before the sweet was served, so Dad helped him to bed.

It had taken Mum all day to prepare the food and lay up the tables, walk us as usual and cook the meal. Although she was pleased with her efforts, it will not be repeated!

January 2005 arrived and Auntie Olive (Dad's sister) came and stayed for ten days to be looked after as she was recovering from a shoulder replacement operation. Mum had to wash her and help her get dressed, cut up her food, etc. etc. Whilst Mum was engaged with her nurse's hat on, Dad walked us. He is usually in bed when we go out in the mornings, so it was rather a shock to his system! Auntie Olive's operation had been cancelled three times, so when she came to stay with us, we were in the middle of having the hall and lounge ceilings replastered! Organised chaos.

When there is time in their busy schedule, we help them in the garden. Dad has made a few flower beds smaller and given us a larger lawn to lie on. Our job is to keep the pigeons away and also the horrid magpies that have wrecked our blackbird nests. Near the fledging time of our blue tits, Solei on three separate occasions raised the alarm at 5.15am to bring Mum rushing through the bungalow, into the conservatory, nightie flapping, waving her arms about to scare the magpies away.

Dad said, "That's a sight to frighten more than the magpies." I just opened one eye and stayed in my bed. It is all very tiring being woken up so early.

We have been kept on our toes the last six months, we still continue to travel over to Uncle Bill's farm at Dane End once or twice a week to keep the farm ticking over, and Bruce is always bathed as he sleeps on Uncle Bill's bed, making it dirty and smelly. Uncle Bill is not at all well and has been diagnosed with terminal lung cancer, so eventually Bruce will have to be found a new home.

We are now pat dogs/carers for Nanny who is eighty-nine years old and Jack, her partner, is eighty-three. Nanny calls him her 'toyboy'. We check on them every day and Mum cooks their meals and Dad walks round to their bungalow with their food on a tray.

Since Christmas, we hadn't seen Simpson for four months or so, and he was proudly brought round to be shown off; wow, he is ginormous! He ran full pelt through the bungalow, using the settees to jump up on to alter direction. I made a rapid retreat to my bed to keep out of the way. Solei challenged him every time he sped by her; he had absolutely no manners at all, barging into Mum giving her bruises. That night Solei dreamed Simpson was jumping on her and she wet her bed during her nightmare.

The next time Simpson came around, he had grown even more, towering above us. He charged around the garden crashing through the flowerbeds like an exocet missile. During his second circuit he tried to jump over me as I was in the way, missed and hit me in my side. I lay there completely winded; Mum rushed over thinking I was dead, but with her help I struggled to my feet and made a beeline for my bed. I am thirteen years old and I should have respect from the yob culture. Once again Solei wet her bed that night. Now Simpson is only allowed here on the lead. He is only eight months old and is six stone worth of solid muscle.

Spring Frolic Day arrived, yippee! I was allowed to go as well as Solei. The dogmobile was made comfy with my duvet and pillow for my head, which is always put in for long journeys, and off we set. The motorway lorry drivers chuckle when they see me in the back. What a beautiful sunny day; we had a lovely time meeting over fifty Beardies and their owners and Solei joined in, playing all the games and as usual flirting with the boys.

July was a very busy time for us. Uncle Bill was taken into hospital with leg ulcers, and it was decided he could no longer live on his farm, so during his hospital stay, time was spent visiting nursing homes in the Hertfordshire area to find somewhere suitable. Uncle Bill's dog, our friend Bruce the Border Terrier, instead of going into kennels was looked after by one of Uncle Bill's carers.

Bruce thought he had gone to heaven. He was walked four miles a day, and spent the evening lying across his new mistress Marianne's feet. They totally loved one another and both were really happy. At the beginning of August, we had a phone call from his new owner. Next door to Bruce's new home lived a cat who often ran through their garden jumping up on the gate teasing Bruce, knowing he couldn't be reached. This particular day, the builders who were working on the house further along had left the gate open, and when the cat shot through to tease Bruce, he ran into the road with Bruce chasing him straight under a car. The cat and our poor friend died instantly. Bruce had three weeks of bliss finding out how he should have been looked after, but now he is over the Rainbow Bridge. Every time we visit the farm now, we really miss our walks with him.

September arrived and Dad actually accompanied us to the Tramps Tuck-In. As usual we had a great time and Mum and Solei enjoyed getting to the finals of the obstacle race, although their team didn't win, Dad was glad he went, just to see Mum making a spectacle of herself, and of course he enjoyed all the lovely grub.

Just before we left for our holiday in Berrynarbor, Combe Martin in Devon, it was a great relief to Mum and Dad to find a good nursing home for Uncle Bill. We also visit him, spending most of our time being 'pat dogs', even being allowed into bedrooms of really poorly people who love dogs to help brighten their day. Uncle Bill is always pleased to see us and sits holding our leads beaming at everyone as if we were his own.

It took us six hours to get to our holiday farm cottage. We stopped twice on the way down, once for us to have a wee and then again for lunch, sheltering under the table keeping out of the hot sunshine. As we are always on our best behaviour we were rewarded with a couple of chips each.

We loved our holiday cottage, called Sloley Farm. Our grooming table was erected in the sunroom and we had three acres of beautifully kept garden to wander around in.

Solei, Annie our fourteen-year-old little brown friend, and I happily settled in (she walks slower than me). After Annie's Mum and Dad and our two-legs had breakfast, we walked down to the picturesque village of Berrynarbor to buy a paper and postcards. We were surprised to find every cottage had a flowerpot man or woman hanging over the walls and off window ledges in various poses and characters. The one holding a catapult was great fun. Of course Mum had to bring one home to put in our garden. Walking back up the very steep hill, we understood why most of the cottages had 'sloley' in their names, as to walk up the hill you could only go slowly.

We drove to Combe Martin in the afternoon and was shocked to find a big notice 'NO DOGS' ON THE BEACH – NOT UNTIL THE 1ST OCTOBER, but further along we found a smaller beach we could use. I had difficulty getting down the steps and Mum and Dad were quite anxious. Mind you, once I was on the sand there was no stopping me, I was off chasing Solei into the water; Annie was quite disdainful trying to pretend she wasn't part of our noisy group. We all slept well that night.

On Sunday we drove to Mortehoe and walked three miles in a round trip to see the Bull Point Lighthouse, returning back along the coastal path climbing forty steep steps up the cliffs. Mum and Dad had to help me, Mum at my front and Dad heaving me up from behind. Annie who is a year older than me managed it very well, but I think I need a hip replacement. We all walked really slowly so Annie and I could recover. Mum was grateful too.

The two-legs had their lunch at 'The Ship Aground' and it smelt delicious; we were allowed small pieces of carrot afterwards. Once back at the farm, we all crashed out and Mum decided that tomorrow we were to have a day's rest. We then found out why they were being so generous – it was some kind of cricket final – so we spent a lazy time being groomed ready to walk down to 'Ye Ole Globe' pub for our evening meal to celebrate winning back the Ashes, whatever they are!

Their plates were loaded with mouth-dribbling food and only Dad finished his meal. Not to upset the chef, Dad used one of our clean poo bags and everyone scraped their plates into it. We lay more than interested in watching their every move, our mouths watering, imagining the culinary delights that were going to be placed before us when we got back home. Wrong – would you believe it – they left without picking up the bag of scraps! Are they senile or what?

We had a great day at Saunton Sands, and hired a beach hut which had chairs and windbreaks so we had shade and shelter from the wind. We all loved the sea and sand, and spent the day in and out of the water. Solei thought it a good idea after swimming to roll in the sand to dry herself. Other holiday makers looked horrified, remarking that they were glad she didn't belong to them.

The next day, we awoke to pouring rain and were taken for a short walk to relieve ourselves; then it was off to Ilfracombe so the two-legs could visit an art exhibition whilst we slept, enjoying the chance to relax in the dogmobile. In the afternoon, the rain cleared and we visited Marwood Gardens, which allowed dogs in on leads. The gardens were vast, many acres with lots of interesting plants, mature trees, bog gardens and ponds. The massive fish in the ponds followed you along and looked like sharks, creating massive waves with their fins showing. We decided not to have a drink or they might have nibbled our noses.

Beardies World

A SANDY SOLEI AND MUFFIN AT SAUNTON SANDS

On the way home, we stopped off at Berrynarbor and visited Miss Muffin's Tea Shop (which I am sure was named after me) for a cream tea. A big cat lay on one of the empty tables and Solei sat totally rigid the whole time we were there, not taking her eyes off it! Oh yes, I must tell you a secret; our two-legs went straight on a diet when they got back home. 'Ye Old Globe' pub had another visit from us, but this time the plates were scraped clean. How they managed it after the cream tea, we don't know. There were many canines sprawled under tables there and we felt the pub owners should have a rosette for allowing us all in there.

The weather forecast was for torrential rain all day Thursday and as we were to be out of our cottage by 10.00am Friday, our two-legs took their time packing and loading up our transport and left after an early lunch. On the way home, we heard Mum and Dad having a post-mortem on the holiday, agreeing it was a lovely area, but too hilly for Annie and me. Solei, of course, loved it all, but our two-legs found it restrictive as there were not many places to visit that allowed us girls.

After four days at home, we were then packing again to spend four days at Uncle Bill's farm. The weather was good and in between our walks we lay outside, keeping guard.

Meanwhile Mum and Dad spent their time sorting through papers and Mum ironing name labels onto Uncle Bill's clothes. We will be returning again soon for Mum to sort the kitchen and Dad to empty the greenhouses.

At Christmas time we will be selling the trees again, then the farm will have to be sold to pay for Uncle Bill's care. At the moment there are no plans for 2006. We will have to be patient and see what transpires.

Joyce Ives

MUFFIN'S LATEST DIARY NOTES – 2006

October and November were quite busy months leading up to Christmas: Uncle Ken, Dad's brother started to spend more time down at the Christmas tree farm, getting things ready for the big rush at Christmas. Uncle Ken had slipped on some icy steps and cracked several ribs, which was the last thing we needed, as it is hard work pushing Christmas trees through the netting.

Mum and Dad's son, Duncan, when hearing our predicament said he would help us the two weekends before Christmas, our busiest time, so Mum busied herself in the kitchen at home, cooking loads of delicious meals, so there would be plenty to eat whilst down on the farm.

We love it when she cooks, the smells wafting across our moist black noses is almost too much to bear, but at our dinner time we usually find some delicious morsel for us in our dishes. Each time we drove over to the farm, Mum put more and more food into the freezer there, soups, dinners, rolls etc. etc.

On the 9th December, we joined Dad down on the farm, and Duncan, Kate, Jordan (Mum and Dad's grandson), and their naughty dog, Simpson the Dobermann, joined us the next day. Simpson stayed with us and Mum whilst the rest of the family worked down in the plantation. Simpson is now two years old, and, me being thirteen, I find him a bit too much to cope with and try to find a corner to lie down and keep out of his way. He is huge, and so solid; when he bumps into Mum, she gets bruises on her legs. Solei isn't too keen either. The only time he ignores us is when Mum takes us all for a walk, when he doesn't bother us and we can then relax. Thank goodness, they only stayed one day, and Solei and I breathed a sigh of relief.

Mum travelled back home with us on the Monday as she had other commitments, and we sadly left poor Dad behind to fend for himself. The 16th December arrived and Mum was packing up again to join Dad down on the farm. This time Duncan, Kate, Jordan and Simpson stayed for the weekend as it was our busiest time. Uncle Ken stipulated that he didn't want any dogs down the yard as parents with their children would be coming to choose their trees and they might be frightened of dogs. It's him that doesn't like dogs!

This was a problem for our Mum, as Simpson doesn't like to be separated from his family and wouldn't stop barking. He was put in the conservatory with his bed and toys to give us a rest from him, but Mum, in the end, let him indoors with us. Whilst she was cooking, she suddenly thought it was all rather peaceful and went into the lounge to find Simpson curled up in Uncle Bill's 'all singing, all dancing chair'. When Simpson saw Mum, hands on hips looking at him, he sat up putting one of his paws on the handset. The look on his face when the chair started to recline, he moved, touching the handset again, the chair then moved forwards to the point of tipping him out. We did admire him though, he still didn't jump off (we would have done) and on moving his position again, his paws caught the handset again, making the chair recline, plus pulsating with a rumbling sound. He had this silly, amused grin on his face, and Mum, trying not to laugh at him, put on her sternest voice, telling him to get off the chair at once. He gave her one of his majestic looks and got down, running into the kitchen, stealing one of the ham rolls that she was preparing to take down the yard to our family of workers.

At the end of the day, and the last of the Christmas tree

shoppers had left, we settled down after being given our dinner, heads on our paws watching as the family settled down to their dinner. Not Simpson though, he is so large that his head rests on the dinner table. He still has no manners, that great long snout of his taking in what was on the table!

It was a really cold weekend and the central heating was playing up, and Mum had electric heaters trying to keep the place warm. She even had the old electric cooker on, all four rings and the oven full blast. She blew the fuses. Dad wasn't pleased of course, and he had to hunt around to fix the fuse box.

Mum had made up the double bed in Uncle Bill's room and had put a blow-up bed on the floor for Jordan. The Ives family junior retired to bed – relief, a bit of peace, we crept onto our duvets and I lowered myself slowly. My arthritis was getting the better of me; I was given medication by the vet, but it hasn't really helped.

Morning dawned, and Kate wandered out of the bedroom complaining they were frozen. Then Duncan wandered out and said he was frozen. He had vacated the double bed for the blow-up bed as Simpson had commandeered it. Solei and I were appalled. Kate and Jordan had to share with Simpson – he had that silly grin on his face again!

Sunday was manic; cars were leaving with their netted trees on their roofs and beaming little two-legs looking forward to Father Christmas coming. The farm was on the market and several people called in to view the property. There were several offers, but the Ives family settled on a lovely family who said they would continue to sell the trees, and had some really good ideas to improve everything.

Christmas was spent at home, and Solei and I were pleased to get back to normal. Dad always walks Solei in the mornings, they go off for a three mile jaunt and Mum and I just walk down the road and back, my poor tired old legs can't go any further. Our vet keeps trying other medication but it makes me ill and I have ended up on a drip twice, which isn't very nice as I am away overnight.

Mum, after reading the article 'Age!' in the *Beardie Times* about hypothyroidism, asked for me to have a blood test as she was rather worried that all my symptoms I have been having might not just be arthritis. The results were quite worrying and I now have an extra tablet called Soloxin. We have to go back in two weeks to see if the levels are right.

After being on the tablets for four days, I didn't really feel much better, although I did surprise Mum in walking a little further in the afternoons. But oh dear, the following morning I didn't feel at all well. Mum helped me into the garden to relieve myself and then she carried me into the lounge and laid me down on some clean bedding. Time passed and I opened my eyes to see my favourite vet standing over me. I gave him one wag of my tail as I recognised his voice. Thank goodness Mum knows how I am feeling. She knelt on the floor and lifted my head and shoulders into her arms, talking gently to me, I licked her hand …

MUFFIN 9.04.92 – 8.05.2006

Joyce Ives

SHE WAS ONLY A DOG
HER STORIES HAVE BEEN TOLD
AND THIS IS HER FINAL CHAPTER

Yes, she was only a dog, but she was ours; she had the sweetest nature, loving, a clown. She could tell the time and an absolute joy to own. We were her guardians for fourteen happy years, and she was guardian to Kizzy and Emma and also Solei's best friend. She has left a huge void in our lives, the time had come to let her go.

>Our best friend closed her eyes
>As her head was in my hand
>The vet said she was in pain
>And it was hard for her to stand.

>The thoughts that scurried through our heads,
>As we cradled her in our arms
>Were of her younger puppy years
>And oh her many charms.

>Today there is not a gentle nudge
>With an intense 'I love you' gaze
>Only a heart that's filled with tears
>Remembering our joy filled days.

>But an angel just appeared to us
>And he said, "You should cry no more!"
>God also loves our canine friends
>He's installed a doggie door!

Muffin, your time with us was full of laughter and wonderful memories.
Joyce and John

MUFFIN IN HER YOUNGER DAYS

Joyce Ives

DEPRESSION

Depression is when I wake up and you are not there
Depression is you not following me around without a care
Depression is walking without you all alone
Depression is just only me chewing a bone.
You left me just as our garden had sprung into life
Without you is like being stabbed with a knife.
Lonely mealtimes with one dish to lick
Oh Muffin, we knew you were sick.
Now my sweet dear friend, you are no longer in pain
Over the Rainbow Bridge is when we meet again.
Love from a distraught
SOLEI

SOLEI LOOKING BACK ON 2006

Muffin, my bestest ever friend who totally mothered me, left us on the 4th May, to join Emma and Kizzy over the Rainbow Bridge. It was my birthday, but we didn't celebrate me being eight years old, we were all too upset. She had always been there for me, on walks when I dashed off into the bushes, she used to sit and wait for me to come out, but I always returned to the pathway further down and she happily tried to slowly catch up with me seeing that I had come to no harm. I have never been left on my own before because when Mum and Dad went out, I had Muffin for company, so now I bark and get upset. At the moment this has been resolved by taking me round to Nanny's bungalow, which is happiness for them and me.

Mum and Dad had a surprise party planned for Nanny's 90th birthday, which helped keep us all busy and took our minds off missing Muffin. It was a good party with relatives and friends I hadn't met before. The caterers requested I be kept out of the kitchen which was difficult because our bungalow is mainly open plan, so, giving them a reproachful look, I settled myself under the drinks table out of the way until they eventually left. Mum and Dad's grandchildren did a martial arts display, so I remained under the table watching their legs and arms going in all directions. Connor who is eight recited a poem and at the end of the entertainment, there was lots of clapping. I felt honoured to be there, because the last party Mum and Dad had, Muffin and me were not included.

At the end of the month, Dad ended up in hospital for a week, which didn't help me one bit. First Muffin leaves me, then Dad disappears; I stuck to Mum like glue and didn't let her out of my sight, unless of course I was taken around to Nanny's when Mum went out.

I had my old friend Annie stay for four days which was nice, but she insisted on sleeping in my cot and not her beanbag. It was good to have her company, although she spent nearly all her time sleeping. Mum tried leaving us for half an hour and on her return I made it clear to her that, although I hadn't barked, I wasn't happy about it.

The beginning of July arrived and I was bathed and prettied up for a day out; chairs were being packed into Dad's car and I followed them around thinking I was going to be left, as I am not allowed in Dad's car, but bless my cotton socks, I could hardly contain my excitement, as my stuff was being packed as well! I gave Dad one of my special hugs, you know, winding my paws around his neck and snuffling under his chin, thank you, thank you. It was Strawberry Tea Day.

We set off early, the air conditioning going full pelt in the car, we arrived much too early and found a space under a large tree for some shade, then walked across the road to the pub for lunch. When we got back we found lots of excited Beardies had arrived, charging about in the sun, but without Muffin, I had no confidence to join in and kept in the shade, saying hello to any Beardies who came to share my water bowl. Mum insisted I entered the musical event, but to our dismay, we were the first to be sent out as I refused to sit! We had a good day though, and Mum presented a cup for 'The Alternative Wet Game' in Muffin's memory, and a few tears were shed. All three of us were choked up.

At the end of the month, Mum started packing for our walking holiday in the Lake District. We left at 5.50am, stopping at a service station for breakfast. As it was too early to arrive at our cottage, we came off the motorway and visited Morecambe Bay. I was disappointed that I was not allowed on the beach, being told it wasn't suitable for me. Apart from the promenade which had been updated, all the shops on the seafront were rundown and really needed a facelift.

We continued our journey and I excitedly sniffed the warm breeze blowing through the windows, the roadside ditches were brimmed full with wild flowers and grasses which bobbed about as we passed by. We eventually arrived at our rented bungalow in Brigsteer, and as there was quite a lot of farm traffic driving through the village, and finding the garden not secure, I had to wait until barriers were found to stop me wandering into the road. The lounge and bedrooms looked out on wonderful scenery, but the garden dropped away dramatically by fifteen feet; I was shown the drop and told to be careful. The bungalow had a wooden balcony off of the lounge, and I loved lying out there looking down into the valley where the cows softly shuffled along, munching on the grass with an odd pheasant or two pecking around the disturbed grass where the cattle's toes had uncovered tasty food for them to eat. A sparrow kept zooming over my head to feed her babies, who were living in a borrowed house martin's nest under the fascia board right by the main bedroom window.

As we had picked the hottest week of the year for our walking holiday, it was decided that the next morning we would get up really early before it got too hot to enjoy our first walk. We drove up to Helsington Barrow to walk Scout Scar. On our Ordnance Survey map it didn't look too long a walk; we would have our breakfast on our return. Well, we walked, and walked, making our way to the viewpoint which at a distance looked like a patio heater, locally called 'the mushroom'. Considering Mum and Dad have been walking for over twenty years, you would think they would have thought to take their sunhats and water, but on reaching 'the mushroom' we watched other people sitting around the circular seating area having their refreshments. One of their comments was:

"You must have had a really early breakfast before you left for this walk!" Mum and Dad were really embarrassed and I was feeling a bit parched.

The 360-degree views were fantastic stretching to the Yorkshire Dales to the East and to the coast on the West. Inside the dome, people were lining up with a metal pole and all around the circumference was written the names of the places where you were looking. We returned on a circular path, Mum commenting that the colour of the lichen on the rocks was an electric green. Was I interested in this? Not at all, but it was a wonderful walk being allowed to run about off my lead, my nose to the ground. Ecstasy. We didn't get our breakfast until 10.40am, unheard of in this family!

For lunch, we drove to 'The Punchbowl' at Crossthwaite, and we sat outside in the shade. My coat had a strange odour as I had brushed past geraniums overhanging the wall. It was all very pretty, tubs of nasturtiums and brightly coloured sun umbrellas. Had it been raining, canines were allowed inside, even though one million pounds had been spent on updating it. (I wonder how many Bonios could be bought for that amount of money?) Mum had herby roast lamb with beautiful mint sauce, and Dad had rabbit pie. I thought rabbits were just for the fun of chasing; I didn't realise they ended up in pies, poor things. They then had white peach Melba and almond ice cream. Everything was homemade, even the ice cream. As usual, I instigate conversation, and we started talking to two very nice people on the next table. We found out that they were farmers, and the lamb that Mum had just eaten was provided by them; having been hung for two weeks, no wonder it was so delicious. From there we drove to Grange over Sands, which we found was no longer sand, but is now a field of grass, so, again, I was disappointed at not having a sandy run.

We decided to go to Kendal on Monday as I needed some shades for my dog mobile; no, not for my eyes, for the windows. I was very grateful when we found some, but going there was a big mistake, as it wasn't very dog-friendly, apart from when

Mum and Dad had lunch outside in a shady courtyard garden and the kind waitress asked if I would like a bowl of water.

On Tuesday, Mum had arranged for us to meet an old school friend whom she hadn't seen since 1963. Her friend Angela and her husband Colin live in Dalton in Furness and, as it was such a lovely day, we were invited to sit in the garden. How wonderful, they were cat lovers. Their first cat soon jumped over the wall to escape me, then I found their second cat. He surprised me by standing his ground, after all it was his garden. Eventually he also beat a hasty retreat and I settled down to snooze in the shade. The chatter went on for what seemed like days, but after numerous cups of tea we all drove off to see the 14th century Dalton Castle.

Angela is the Keeper of the Keys, so we were given our own private viewing – it is only open on Saturdays. We were even locked in to stop people following us, and Angela wrote in the Visitors' Book '2 people, one dog'. It didn't smell too musty, but it was lovely and cool. The door was unlocked into the guard room housing many treasures. Angela also unlocked many of the display cases and Mum and Dad were allowed to handle some of the artefacts. Do you like Dad and me proudly showing the Scottish 16th century basket handle sword and 16th century shield made out of leather, called a targ? We were so privileged.

We were shown the dungeons, and I popped my head down the hole in the floor; Mum was holding on to me tightly in case I fell in as I quivered with excitement imagining how awful it must have been to have been shut in down there with no fresh air or light.

After stumbling up a narrow, left-handed spiral staircase (normally they go right handed), I soon realised I had to keep to the widest part, after slipping a couple of times. Angela unlocked the door at the top and we walked into a bright courtroom, large beams of sunlight flooding onto the floor. Hanging on the main wall was restored 16th century armour, but there wasn't any men inside them. We admired a beautifully carved wooden lectern and many display boards with prints of George Romney paintings. No, we hadn't heard of him either, but I did try to look interested. We turned to see four wooden chairs butted up alongside each other. Keith Alexander was the sculptor who had made and carved the chairs displaying medieval punishment.

The first chair had a fish in a ducking stool. The stool was for gossiping and scolding women. The fish represented fish being sold on the large slab which still stands outside the castle. The second chair had a sheep in a pillory and represented the money that the Abbey made from selling the wool. The third chair had a goose on a whipping post, which depicted Goose Green, where the boys looked after the geese just below the castle.

I stood there more than a little bored, but as I looked at the fourth chair, horror of horrors, on this one was carved a dog hanging from a gibbet, Angela looked down at me and said, "This one depicts what happens to dogs who kill sheep." I will not forget that fourth chair.

After locking up, we walked down the hill to Goose Green to have some lunch. I lay under the table reflecting on sheep-killing by dogs. I think our species are shot if it happens, aren't they? From there, we drove to Furness Abbey ruins (English Heritage). What a good day we were having. Dogs were allowed in the grounds off the lead. I have never heard so much chatter and when they sat in the shade, I gladly lay down for a rest. Taking Angela and Colin back to their home, we said our goodbyes, delighted to be told what a wonderfully behaved Beardie I was, but I couldn't wait to get home for a well earned rest in a cool spot as it was still intolerably hot.

Another day dawns and Mum took me out early for a short walk, a sheep had got out of one of the fields, and with that fourth chair in mind, I surprised myself by helping Mum to guide the hissing sheep back under the metal gate to join her very joyful lamb. Dad says sheep do not hiss, only snakes, but Mum and I know different! Breakfast demolished, we drove to Lakeside, Newby Bridge, just in time to catch a cruise ship sailing to Bowness. This was a new experience for me and I managed to tuck myself under the wrinklies bench, keeping in the shade. The rumble of the ship's engines went right through my body, which made me tremble, but half an hour into the journey, I became used to it – but really pleased to get on terrafirma again. We had an hour or so before we could get a ship back, so keeping to the shady side of the shops, we wandered around the touristy area. Back on board, we managed to find a walkway in the shade with a cooling wind blowing through my coat to return to Lakeside. Several people came over and gave me a stroke, but that of course made me even hotter.

On arriving home, we climbed down the terraced garden to a flat piece of lawn and tried to cool off under the shade of a huge sycamore tree, I could hear rustlings and creepings from the hedgerow, but was too tired to investigate. I awoke to find that Mum and Dad were getting harassed by little black bugs, so we had to walk back up to our very hot bungalow.

The next morning we awoke to rain coming down in stair rods which was very welcome as it reduced the oppressive heat. Dad and I took a twenty-minute walk and got soaked. On returning I was quickly dried off with my hairdryer before we settled down to breakfast. It wasn't long before the sky lightened and we drove over to the Grizedale Centre Forest Park. We had found a map at our holiday bungalow and Mum wanted to follow one of the sculpture trails. We had a choice of easy, moderate or strenuous, and I was quite surprised when they picked a moderate one.

At first, it was quite easy climbing, but the sun wasn't out then. We stopped for a break – I was grateful for a bowl of water and half a Bonio. Carrying on, we passed a fantastic riveted metal sculpture of two naked tin men, one suspended, being pulled on a rope by the other. Mum was absolutely fascinated and took a couple of photos. I wonder if it had anything to do with the naked form? By now the sun had come out and, with us leaving the shelter of the forest, we started to slow up and even I was plodding along. We cut the walk short and only did two and a half miles. Fortunately the return journey was mostly downhill.

We drove to the Grizedale Centre and had lunch, and a rest in the shade. There is so much to do: cycling (there is a bike hire shop), orienteering courses, guided walks, an adventure playground for your little two-legs, and high ropes adventure (Go Ape) for your larger two-legs – they have to wear a harness, so they can't fall out of the trees!

In the evening, we drove to Underbarrow to another pub called 'The Punchbowl' for dinner. I thoroughly enjoyed the evening as lots of staff and other people came and gave me a cuddle. Of course we always have to correct them when they think I am an Old English sheepdog. Unbelievable.

Our last day dawned, and this time we are glad it is cloudy. We walked from the cottage, climbing steeply across the fields, I happily ran around, smelling scraps of fur, feather and small bleached bones near to where I could see a fox's lair in an earthy hollow under the gorse. I heard Mum and Dad calling, so I backed out, taking care not to get my coat caught in the brambles, to catch them up. At the local church we took a water and Bonio break. The path gradually descended to Sizergh Castle. Dad was glad he was following the Ordnance Survey map or we would never have found it. The footpath took us directly into the castle grounds, it was deserted and we wandered around the beautiful gardens. As we were leaving we did notice a lady looking at us and felt that we shouldn't be there. Heads down and following our map, not looking back at the lady, we likened ourselves to deer knowing they have been spotted, and quickly melted into the countryside towards Brigsteer again. We noticed that they were building tea rooms and a new car park, then realised that the castle was closed to visitors while all these new major works were being carried out. We wondered why there was no one to pay! Getting back on track, we found ourselves descending a very steep path that Mum and Dad could only get down backwards. I grinned to myself waiting patiently at the bottom – it is better to have four legs!

We managed at last to find the wide track that we wanted which would lead us eventually back to Brigsteer, but was stopped by a friendly farmer and his dog in the biggest tractor I have ever seen asking if we were lost. Dad said he knew exactly where we were and showed him on our map. He then said the track we were on was not a public right of way and suggested we went back up the footpath through the woods and walked along the road which would have added another one and a half miles to our journey. After telling him what trouble we had climbing down, to try to get back up would be practically impossible for my elderly guardians. He laughed and said he had no objection to us taking the track but couldn't vouch for the other farmers and confirmed with us it would only take about half an hour before we reached the road.

We spent about ten minutes or so chatting to him and mentioned ticks and asked if his collie was bothered by them. We were surprised to hear there were no ticks in the area we were in; when they renew their stock, they bought tick-free animals. Farmers over the other side of Scout Scar had sheep with ticks and bought in sheep with ticks. He said if you put tick-free sheep in a tick area, they would die as they would not be immune. We walked on with this new knowledge in our brains, enjoying the peace and tranquillity until we were suddenly confronted with about 150 sheep being driven down the track towards us. Mum and Dad hurriedly found a safe place behind a metal gate standing against the hedge hoping they wouldn't see us as they were driven to pastures new. I have never heard so many different bleating sounds, high, middle and low pitched, a few looked at us but walked slowly passed, what a terrible noise they made. We were soon on our way again, grateful to be on the metal road climbing back up to our cottage. I threw myself down for a snooze. We had walked about five miles and it took us two-and-three-quarter hours.

I thought we were in for the evening as Mum and Dad had started packing, keeping clothes back for the following day, but no, we were off out again, meeting some other friends who they hadn't seen since 1992. Mum and Dad with their first two beardies, Kizzy and Emma, stayed with them in Ulverston for a week's walking holiday. Early the next morning, Dad packed the dogmobile with our luggage; we had eaten most of our food, so I had more room in the back whilst Mum had a clean up (she always does as she feels it should be left as we expect to find it).

Reflecting on our holiday, we were not too happy with the cottage. The oven door fell off twice, which was quite dangerous; the microwave sounded like a tractor going by; the shower head was held together with three elastic bands and the bathroom sink was so low, you could have used it as a footbath, but you couldn't fault it for the beautiful views, that is if you could see out of the windows which hadn't been cleaned for at least a year.

On our way home, we had advance warning of a big traffic jam at Birmingham, and with me in mind, because of the heat Mum and Dad took the toll road. They said it was worth it. There were no hold-ups and we highly recommend it.

Home again life continued as normal, but I heard rumours that Mum and Dad are going off by themselves for two weeks and I shall be boarding with my Beardie friends I will be looking forward to their company and having a race about with them.

For some time now, I haven't felt so well, even before we lost our beloved Muffin, so we became quite well known at our vets as they struggled to make me better. I was feeling so lethargic, and had constant tummy aches, which improved with antibiotics, but then quickly returned. I had a test for Addison's as Mum felt that a lot of my symptoms pointed to this, but it came back negative. More blood tests and then the final one showed up I was very ill. By this time I had stopped eating and my stomach wouldn't even tolerate fish and rice.

We were referred to a specialist vets over in Higham Gobian, Hertfordshire as there were no appointments to be had at the Royal Veterinary College and after an hour's interview and being prodded about, I was led outside to a large building, my collar and lead taken off and a rope noose put around my neck – oh gawd, no, no, I am not a sheep killer! I was led away and I turned to look anxiously at Mum and Dad to see Mum sobbing in Dad's arms.

The nurse who looked after me was very nice and the next day I had all my beautiful fur on my tummy shaved off. This, I was told, was for an ultrasound. I was allowed some food later as I was quite hungry, but the following day, I was starved. I could hear other patients being fed but why not me? Oh dear, another day dawns and my other leg was shaved, more needles and I don't remember quite what happened, but then I had the most enormous tummy ache and it was really embarrassing as I couldn't stop going to the toilet. I was most unhappy. The day after, still no grub, and again after another needle, I was taken into an operating theatre. When I came round I was back in my kennel again and being offered food.

After five days there, I was led out of the building to see Mum and Dad's best friends, Barbara and Mike, who are Annie's guardians. I was so pleased to see them and couldn't wait to jump into the back of their car. I heard them being told I had inflammatory bowel disease, but the veterinary specialists were still waiting for the results of some biopsies to make sure there was no cancer.

Arriving home, I rushed in and ran around the bungalow looking for Mum and Dad. For goodness sake, where were they? Barbara, Mike and Annie, settled down for the evening and then they said goodnight to us both and unbelievably got into Mum and Dad's bed. No one is allowed to sleep in their bed but them, they would be in trouble when Mum and Dad got home. The next morning, we were taken for a walk, then my new bag of food, medicines, and my duvet were packed into the car; off we drove to Annie's bungalow. I knew what had happened: I had been so much trouble, I had been abandoned! Early evening, I was again in the car with all my belongings and taken over to my Beardie friends.

After the usual pleasantries of saying hello, I soon settled down with my new family that rescued me, although I was not happy at being given my liquid medicines. I absolutely hated the Zantac. I enjoyed my stay and loved sharing the walks with my friends, although I couldn't believe Mum and Dad had abandoned me just because I cost a mere £2,000. I really missed them. Time had not dragged at all, and one evening the back door opened and in walked my beloved guardians.

Oh absolute joy, I gave them both a paws-around-the-neck hug and snuggly kisses; we all sat down and they had cups of tea, a faint aroma of suntan oil wafting under my nose as they caught up with all the news hearing that my biopsies were clear. After more hugs and kisses, we left for home.

Now I am on my new diet and with the change of medication, I am now enjoying life again and looking forward to my next adventure.

A LETTER HOME from KIRI

5th May 2007

Dear Mummy and Daddy,

I am just writing down my experiences, so you will know never to leave me here again. I thought we were just visiting, but you went off leaving me behind, so I lay down where I last saw you by the back door. I soon got tired of waiting and decided to explore, following my adopted Mum around, not letting her out of my sight. Then I heard her calling me, my adopted Dad joined in too, their voices calling my name, getting ever more frantic. I had only been here an hour; I was supposedly lost, both of them yelling their heads off.

Silly them, I was quietly sitting in the dog's bathroom, I had followed my new Mum in there and as that was where my food was I had lingered and had got shut in. They were very pleased to see me. Poor old pensioners, they went off looking for the whisky bottle, as they were so traumatised.

When it came to bed time I was a very good girl and settled down straight away. My new friend Solei was very relieved, I don't know why, because every time I went to her she was always grinning and showing her teeth.

MONDAY

New Mum let me out of my crate, oh joy! I bounced all over my new friend, I found she didn't like that much, so every morning after that, I was let out in the garden on my own. I had a lovely walk with my new parents in Penn Wood, and Solei too, she kept running off to chase squirrels and I of course followed, but returned almost immediately as I didn't want to get lost. In the afternoon I crashed out in the garden for forty-five minutes and didn't wake up until I was called for my supper. I always gobble my meal up in seconds but quickly learned to respect Solei's dish of food, and now stand beside her instead of getting my head in her bowl while she is eating.

TUESDAY

Another lovely walk; same woods, but a different area. My guardians had a visitor today. I have noticed that they always keep the doors to the hall and the bedrooms closed, but their visitor didn't know this and I found one door to the hall open.

Wow, new territory! I marked the carpet with an enormous wee that had the wrinklies dancing around with kitchen roll etc. Was this a problem? I am still making my presence felt by 'sounding off' at new sounds, I puff myself up and prance on four stiff legs. It is enough I think to scare anybody – including myself.

WEDNESDAY

I am well into my new routine, and feeling more at home. I slept for an hour and a half this morning, giving everyone a well earned break. We had another new walk, which I enjoyed as Solei chased her ball and I could nearly keep up with her. New Mum can't understand why I wait until I get home to do my wees and poos and not while I am out during my walks, never mind!

Solei took me round to visit her Nanny and Jack. They were very pleased to see me, another place and garden to check out. I must have been good because they said they looked forward to seeing me again.

THURSDAY

Solei still doesn't like me much, I wouldn't leave her alone today and I ended up with a sore muzzle. Still, when we are out for our lovely walks we get along okay. I enjoy gardening too and Solei has taught me to chase the pigeons away. It is my new game.

FRIDAY

I woke new Mum up at 5.40am this morning. It wasn't until later she realised that she hadn't drawn the blinds in the conservatory. We went on a short walk and then later we went on a longer walk with a new friend called Gemma, a Goldie. She liked playing with me, but I knocked her over and rolled over too. We were both covered in dust and twigs. Poor Gemma, she is only two, but she nearly died of meningitis last year, which has weakened her back legs. She is three times my size, I don't know my own strength.

We all went to a place called a pub and we four-legs lay in the shade whilst the two-legs ate their meal and chatted. Solei and I had our lunch too.

SATURDAY

Great fun, Henry and Joseph came round to help us in the garden. I enjoyed pinching all the clippings and hiding them. I even pinched one of the pot stands. New Dad was not amused. He also wasn't very pleased when he found a lump of soil on the dining room carpet all chewed up. He has got a hoover, hasn't he?

I have now learned what to do on walks now. When Solei did a poo today, I proudly assumed the position right beside her and did one too! I weed on the walk as well. I was highly praised and new Mum said this is progress. In the afternoon, whilst new Mum was quietly reading the paper, every time I heard one of the neighbours working in their gardens I 'sounded off' time and time again until she threatened me with her newspaper saying she didn't want to be served with an ASBO. Whatever that means.

Solei delightedly told me that I am going home tomorrow. She says she can't wait to get some peace and quiet.

With love and licks from your dear six-month-old Bearded Collie,
Kiri

SOLEI

EXTRACTS FROM SOLEI'S DIARY 2007

Since my 'Travelogue' in autumn 2006, this year has been extremely busy. The February half term holidays arrived and whilst Mum and Dad took their three grandsons away aged twelve, ten and eight to Wookey Hole and Cheddar Gorge for four days, I stayed with my elderly brown friend, Annie. Dogs are allowed at Cheddar Gorge, but the decision was made to leave me behind. Auntie Barbara took me on some lovely long new walks, although Annie, who was not well, took very small walks with Uncle Michael. It was the first time I had spent nights at Annie's and was told I was a very good girl and was no trouble apart from them having to wash my paws. They even brushed me!

A few weeks later I was so upset to hear my little brown friend Annie was put to sleep as she was so poorly. Whenever I visit her home now, I have stopped looking for her and just settle down remembering all the great holidays we shared and fun times we had when we were both younger.

Sadly, Uncle Bill, Dad's brother, died on 17th February, this means we no longer travel to the nursing home. I am sure Uncle Bill's four dogs who loved him during their lives met up with him over the Rainbow Bridge.

I wasn't allowed to go to Uncle Bill's funeral, but I have been promised I can visit his local church, which is on a hillside overlooking Bill's Christmas tree farm, where he used to live. His ashes have been interned under a beautiful yew tree.

Nanny, who is 90, became ill a couple of days later and was taken into hospital for an overnight stay, which turned into six weeks throwing us all into turmoil and my usual routine was shot to pieces. She was fitted with a pacemaker and, once stabilized eventually sent home. During this time we had to have the electricians in to completely rewire and earth her bungalow as the old wiring might have affected her pacemaker.

April arrived and on one glorious Saturday morning, Mum and me were walking in my favourite woods. I love Mum taking different paths each time we go there. We had only been walking ten minutes and I turned round after hearing a thump to find Mum flat on her face. She didn't get up straight away and I had to sit beside her whilst she recovered, brushing the soil off her nose. There was nobody around as it was only 7.00am, most people have a lie in on a Saturday! After speaking to Dad on her mobile, she eventually got up and told me she was sorry, but we had to go back to the dogmobile and return home. I was a bit upset as normally we are out walking for over an hour.

Mum drove home really slowly and each corner we came to I heard Mum groaning as she tried to change gear. Dad was waiting for us and I was quickly dunked in the dog bath to clean me up, then taken directly to Nanny and Jack's where I had my breakfast. Dad took Mum to hospital and thankfully, because it was so early, was the first to be seen. She had broken her left wrist damaging the tendon leading to her thumb where the break was.

Poor Dad had six weeks coping with Mum in plaster and a sling, walking me and doing all the things that Mum couldn't do one-handed. During this time I had to endure Dad grooming me, but he learned very fast following Mum's instructions; he did tug a bit but I am sure sometimes he made me look even more beautiful than when Mum groomed me!

One evening I was lying snoozing in my bed – well, I am now nine years old and I do need more sleep – when I suddenly had a bundle of black fur throw herself on top of me, all mouth and paws. I was so shocked, I couldn't get away from her; wherever I moved my head this tornado was in my face. This unruly six-month old baby Beardie called Kiri was staying for a week, they could have warned me, what a nightmare. Thank goodness she slept in her crate at night, giving me some peace. For the whole week I tried to keep out of her way without much success, but going for walks with her was happiness for both of us. It was like being a family again when I had my dear old friend Muffin to walk with. As Mum couldn't drive, Dad came too. I quite enjoyed having Kiri following me when I dashed off chasing the squirrels. It seemed very strange and quiet when she went home.

May arrived and Mum was kindly given a lift to the Spring Frolic as she wanted to learn about the Tellington Touch. She told Dad later she was very impressed and said if there was an opportunity to attend again, she would like to go. When Dad and I arrived because of the rain, the games were held in the village hall. What's a bit of rain to a Beardie? I wandered around checking out all the baby Beardies, but was disappointed Kiri wasn't there.

In July, I was happy to meet Kiri again when I stayed with her and her Beardie family whilst Mum and Dad travelled to Spain to spend a week with Mum's brother and wife who emigrated out there two years ago. I enjoyed the extra canine company and had fun on my walks winding up my mates. Dad returned home feeling poorly and ended up in hospital for a couple of days. He had contracted viral pleurisy.

It is now the end of July and I'm lying curled up in my comfy quilt looking around me. The situation here isn't one I have experienced before, but being a Beardie I take on new challenges quite easily, as long as I am fed, walked, groomed and cuddled, which as you all will agree are the necessities in life. Anything else that happens, I can cope with.

My bed is in the conservatory and there isn't much room in here for me to walk around and lie down, other than in my bed. Mum is lying on the settee with a poorly right paw, her big claw and foot in a splint and wrapped up in bandages, propped up on pillows (something about a bunion) her crutches leaning against the settee. Once again poor old Dad has 'to do it all'. Normally it is quite roomy in here, but there are ladders, buckets, my grooming table, lots of bin liners stuffed with my towels, walking boots etc.

My bathroom at the end of the conservatory had been emptied out and the builders have insulated and plastered the walls and ceiling. What was wrong with it as it was, I don't know, but Mum and Dad have told me, instead of the old plasterer's bath that Dad converted many years ago, a butler sink is being fitted, to bathe me and for paw washing. I am going to feel like a princess. Does that mean we will have a butler? There is nowhere for him to sleep and he isn't having my bed. I will now have to share it with the washing machine and tumble dryer, but hey, I will have a lovely big sink to be cleaned up in, but I will need a rubber bath mat or I might slip.

I really feel like protesting; the bungalow has become a builder's yard, new windows and doors, the kitchen has been ripped out, boxes everywhere. I had plenty of attention from the men and not much time for snoozing. All that noise was deafening. At last things started to settle down and it is now the end of September. Wow, where has this year gone? Oh, they have packed boxes again and suitcases, it is my time at last, my holiday, they always give me a walking holiday away somewhere once a year, I really thought they had forgotten in all the upheaval. Mum told everybody that I have to have a holiday or I wouldn't have anything to write in my diary.

We had a good journey across to Norfolk and eventually travelled down narrow roads to Upton village, my quivering nose registered that we were in horse country, and we stopped outside a pretty cottage built in 1861 which had been renovated by the owners who lived next door.

What a lovely lady, she had baked a cake and even provided dog towels for me. When Mum grabbed the watering can after I did a wee on the magnificent lawn, she told us she wasn't bothered about dead patches!

The cottage was beautifully decorated and furnished; one of the doors in the kitchen opened directly onto curved stairs that went up very steeply and had just a rope on the wall which Mum and Dad precariously hung on to get to the top. To descend, they would cling onto the rope and walk down backwards. At bedtime I was not at all happy when I was left downstairs, and moaned and groaned and yipped. I was told time and time again to 'settle down – be quiet'. None of us got any sleep. I heard Mum telling Dad that I would soon get used to my new surroundings.

Sunday morning, we drove to Buxton to meet up with some friends, Philip and Mary, who Mum and Dad met on holiday last year in Majorca. I was allowed to wander around the kitchen, laundry room and conservatory. Oh my, I found a strong pungent aroma on the cushions which spelled out CAT. She was not around; unknown to me, she had been put upstairs out of harm's way! After the two-legs demolished tea, coffee and beautiful homemade scones, which were put directly under my nose on the coffee table – one look from Dad told me not to touch (my manners were perfect as I resisted the temptation) – we then travelled to the National Trust Cley Centre, where it was heaving with twitchers watching the birds. A rare one had arrived to feed and the cars were nose to tail as word had got out, all rather boring for me.

Lunch had been booked at 'Cookies'. It is open every day apart from Christmas Day and you always have to book. Their premises alongside their house consisted of a sun chalet, a wet weather plastic gazebo and tables and chairs outside. It was all very quirky and packed with two-legs and some four-legs enjoying every fish dish imaginable. We were in the gazebo, which was more than cosy! From there, we then drove to Blakeney Hotel (a bit posh) where we sat out on the veranda (dogs not allowed inside), and – would you believe it – they then got stuck into tea, sandwiches and tea cakes. I enjoyed all the fussing and cuddles from people at other tables. I just loved all the attention.

By the time we got back to our cottage, it was time for bed, oh dear, they went up those stairs again, leaving me at the bottom on my duvet and the door open, but access denied to me. With the door open I knew they could hear me, of course they didn't get much sleep again, I was so unhappy, I knew they were up there as they kept bellowing down to me to be quiet! In the morning a bleary-eyed Dad walked me down to the paper shop; then, after breakfast we just sat around, my guardians discussing what they were going to do with me as I hadn't settled. I listened intently; they were talking about going home!

It was decided I needed a good walk, so with Ordnance Survey map in hand, we left for Upton Marshes. We had only been walking twenty minutes when we found a giant digger shoring up the defences to stop the River Bure from flooding over. There were signs telling us to use a temporary footpath, which we took. The blackberries were hanging like grapes which Mum and Dad feasted on. Following the new signs we had a difficult journey to the dyke, arriving at the river inlet where lots of boats were moored. The three of us got very muddy, but luckily the landlord of 'The White Horse' allowed us in, giving me a large bowl of water and said that dogs were better than humans. Of course I had to agree. I was transfixed by a parrot on top of his cage doing a dance calling 'hello' repeatedly to me. It was the biggest bird I have ever seen.

That night I again voiced my concerns that I was downstairs on my own. In the morning I was getting black looks; I was so traumatised that I stopped eating and kept trying to bury my food bowl under a pile of towels.

Oh great, we are off out again, this time to Winterton-on-Sea. DOGS ALLOWED ALL YEAR ROUND. After a cup of tea at the spotless Winterton Gap Café (dogs allowed in on leads), we turned left down onto the sands and walked to Winterton Ness. It was cloudy and very windy, so we climbed up the sand dunes and down out of the wind where it was lovely and warm. I loved this walk up and down the hills; I found loads of rabbit holes, but didn't see those furry creatures.

By the time we got back to the friendly café, it was lunchtime with Mum and Dad downing ham, egg and chips and me happily eating my breakfast because I didn't eat it earlier. The sun came out and we decided to turn right and walk the sands to Memsby. The wind was whipping the waves into froth and I darted about trying to catch the bubbles as they blew across the beach. It started to get late and we had to find a gap between the cliffs to get through to the valley area to walk back to the café. This time it was lovely and flat. Mum's pedometer said we had walked seven miles.

AT MEMSBY

The volunteer coastguards allowed us into an exhibition showing all their artefacts which had been washed up on the beach which included a photograph of a prickly (like a hedgehog) tropical puffer fish, seventeen inches long. Portugal was the nearest sighting before this one was found. Mum was asked if she could identify an object covered in barnacles. Studying it she said it was handcuffs, and she was right! Mum and Dad had walked fourteen miles. I am proud to announce I did far more.

You would think by now I was really tired, but that night after an hour of singing, I was allowed up in their bedroom; totally against the rules, but we all got a good night's sleep.

We visited Fairhaven Woodland and Water Garden where dogs are allowed on leads. A visit here would be better in the spring and summer. We took a boat ride on an Edwardian-style cruiser, which was completely boring for me. I was very muddy, so wasn't allowed to sit on Mum's lap to see out. We sailed as far as St. Benet's Abbey which was a huge ruin used by monks in days gone by.

SEE, I GOT MY WAY AT LAST

Joyce Ives

NOT MY IDEA OF FUN

Once back at the cottage, Mum bucketed me; out came the shampoo and the afternoon was spent grooming me, as that evening we were off to Philip and Mary's for a BBQ to meet their family. I finally met their cat, who strolled under the table not realising I was there. She was soon whisked away. I was totally unconcerned, after all I knew it was her house! We had a very happy evening, lots of laughing and jollity. We left quite late to be confronted with dense fog. It took us forty minutes to get there but nearly two hours to find our way back.

We found Cromer not to our liking; the tide was in, so we travelled to Mundesley. Mum tried to walk me along the coast but there were wooden defences all shored up and each beach was sectioned off so we came back. The wind was very cold but it was sunny.

On our last day, we started at Upton Dyke to try a leisurely circular walk through lovely quiet marshes and into woodland making our way to the River Thurne meeting up with the

Weavers Way Walk, which had beautiful views of the river and boats. The people waved at us as they sailed by. We eventually arrived at Acle Bridge and the boating marina where you can hire boats for a holiday. In the olden days the bridge had three arches and a murky past as it was used to hang smugglers and wrong-doers who had upset the Lord of the Manor. The now-new metal bridge takes the A47 to Great Yarmouth.

Crossing this very busy road, we continued alongside the river, turning off at Acle Dyke, which was being renovated and had to cross the A1064 – even harder to do, the oldies had to break into a run! Walking through Acle village we picked up another footpath to Fishley, a very small village consisting of one pub and one church. Onwards across sugar beet fields to 'The White Horse' again to be met with another bowl of water whilst the two-legs tucked into their fish and chips. We had walked six miles.

Hurrah, we were home now and I had never been so pleased to get back, I threw myself onto my bed and slept blissfully upside down, snoring my block off for hours. Happiness is coming home but also going away; a bungalow next time Mum, not a house.

2008 – WILL I EVER LIVE A NORMAL LIFE?

After my Norfolk holiday last year, I thought my guardians' lives would improve, but Mum once again took to sitting around for another six weeks after one more operation. Christmas was spent quietly.

Just to remind you, I still continued to pick at my grub and couldn't really care if I went for a walk or not. I had a nail bed infection and the vet made Mum cut all the fur off my feet as he said I was sure to get another sore nail. The first antibiotics didn't help so a swab was taken which showed up that there was yeast present. A blood test revealed that I had raised cholesterol. As I am on a low fat diet, our vet believed that I might have a thyroid problem and another blood test proved he was right. I am now on Soloxine, making me a very happy bouncing girl and the squirrels have to watch out but I still can't catch them.

Goodness gracious, what is the matter with my guardians? Now Dad has been in hospital and it was Mum's turn to run around after Dad for six weeks. I gave up on expecting Dad to walk me and my allegiance, of course, turned to Mum for all my needs.

Guess where I went the other Sunday – Mum took me to church to gather in honour of Saint Francis of Assissi to give thanks for looking after us animals. Over 60 two-legs attended with their pets to be blessed.We shared a pew with a black

Labrador called Jet and a very sweet long haired Dachshund who enjoyed sniffing my ears. The hymn singing lulled me to sleep and I found one of the plush red hassocks on the floor a very comfortable pillow. Behind us sat a Lurcher and two pretty Belgium Bantams. Us animals were very good, but the children there were noisily excited so I didn't hear everything the vicar was saying. I pricked up my ears, though, when he asked if anybody had brought snakes, cavies, hamsters, gerbils or crustaceans, and seemed a little disappointed to find the congregation consisted mostly of dogs.

I looked around, all the two-legs were laughing and smiling, showing their teeth: this is so strange, it means they are happy, but when we show our teeth it is because we are angry and warning people away. We might share many genes, but we are very opposite in this respect.

We had a pet parade, each of us was asked our name and blessed individually. The largest animal was a Ridgeback; the oldest dog was fourteen; I also saw three cats, two rabbits and the smallest creature was a snail in a jam jar! We didn't quite hear what the snails name was – maybe it was called Slimey! Mum blesses snails but not in that way as snails turn her hostas into lace.

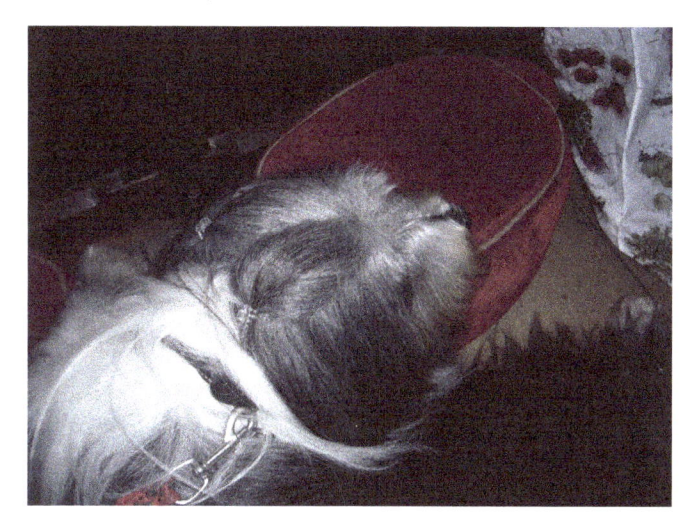

JUST THE RIGHT HEIGHT ... LOVELY

I, myself, caused quite a stir and everyone who spoke to us said how clean and pretty I was, and what breed?

At least nobody thought I was an Old English Sheepdog. They didn't believe Mum when she explained I was quite a normal dog getting plastered in mud and rolling in anything smelly!

May arrived and once again the household was in turmoil. Nanny who is ninety-two went into hospital for a complete knee operation. Unfortunately, although the sides of the bed were holding her in, she managed to shuffle down to the bottom of the bed and fell out onto the floor getting her arm trapped in one of the sides and bruising all down the side of her operated knee and leg. What with the anaesthetic and the morphine, she was agitated and confused. That day, during the visiting time, Mum stayed five hours trying to keep her calm and stopping her from climbing out of bed.

When a totally traumatised Mum came home after visiting Nanny, bursting through the door, she asked Dad if he had remembered to give me my thyroid pill. He had forgotten. Normally I am given my pill at 7.00pm and as Mum has to take a pill in the evening too, we always have them at the same time. She was in such a state worrying about Nanny, she swallowed my pill by mistake!

Dad got on the phone to the emergency vet and he said he couldn't help as Mum was a human, so Dad phoned the emergency out of hours doctor. He asked Mum's weight and height and other medical details. He said he would phone back as soon as he had got an answer from the Poisons Unit. After about fifteen minutes he phoned and said that Mum was not in too much danger but might get heart palpitations, which she did get later on but only lasted about an hour.

I am beginning to wonder if it is safe to be living with these two old people. Whilst eating their dinner with friends, telling them the drama, these were a few comments that were made:

"Is she barking mad?"

"At least you will know when she is happy now because her tail will wag."

"Are you sure you don't want a Bonio for your dinner?"

"Does she keep rolling over on her back asking for her tummy to be tickled?"

"Do you have to take her out with Solei for her last wee before they go to bed?"

Mum is embarrassed typing this up for me, but has taken the joking in good heart.

I am being taken to a bungalow near Stogumber in Somerset early October for MY HOLIDAY! The owners have two acres of lawn at the front and a pond with a rowing dinghy and a trout stream in a beautiful woodland glade. I will put paw to paper on my return to let you know my adventures.

Joyce Ives

MUM

MY OCTOBER 2008 WALKING HOLIDAY (Well, sort of!)

Hi everybody, it is me again, as promised I thought I would keep you up to date with my adventures staying near Stogumber in Somerset.

We had a good journey down on Friday and I had a good view out of the window as there was so much packed under me, my head almost reached the roof of the car! Leaving the motorway, we drove down very narrow lanes with no passing places and on a couple of occasions either us or the vehicle we met had to reverse back to an adjoining road to let the other through. The windows were kept up because the hedgerows were flicking into the car. Driving over a railway bridge we noticed lots of men standing around with cameras mounted on tripods.

Eventually we arrived at big brown double gates and, once opened, I could see doggie paradise. The huge, well-manicured lawns rolled down to the fast flowing Doniford Stream that snaked its way through the lovely grounds. Cattle and sheep grazed on the lower hills and we could see the Quantocks in the distance.

No one was there to greet us but we found the key under the mat at the entrance to our compact 'granny annexe'. It was warm and cosy. I checked out all the rooms, which didn't take long as it was a very small place. I was surprised to find that the shower curtain had lots of happy green frogs, some wearing pink spotted bow ties laughing down at me.

Joyce Ives

Whilst Mum started to unpack, Dad took me to explore the grounds, passing through a gate into woodland with a narrow-stepped pathway which wound down to a clearing. Wow, a beautiful sunhouse, a barbeque area and a large lake with a little rowing boat moored near the landing stage. I thought it would be fun to jump into it, but quickly noticed there was rainwater in the bottom, so decided I wouldn't be Dad's best Beardie if I did.

Back at the bungalow, we met a lovely lady called Jenny who was looking after the owner's two very friendly Labradors, and three Jack Russell Terriers belonging to her. Every morning one of the Labradors lay on the lawn outside our bungalow waiting for me to go out and play with him.

Toot, toot, rumble rumble, clackity clack, clackity clack, what was that noise? I was quite frightened and jumped up looking around me, seeing nothing and then silence. Mum said to me, "It's alright, Solei, it is a big steam train." So that was why all those men were waiting around with cameras. The West Somerset Railway Line ran right behind our bungalow. It was a special weekend when train buffs congregated and rode in the carriages being pulled by lots of different types of steam trains. Even one had been shipped in from America. The railway line was so close to the back of our bungalow that the people hanging out of the windows waved to Mum when she was in the kitchen.

The next morning Mum and Dad didn't wake up until 7.00am. What is this, you would think they were on holiday!

It doesn't mean they can change my routine. I expect my thyroid pills at 7.00am, so Mum crawled out of bed yawning and padded into the kitchen to get my pills and breakfast. Dad showered and then he and I went off to explore; he found a footpath across the road that ran alongside the railway line. We walked a couple of miles to Stogumber Railway Station passing through lots of gates and back again. My paws were covered in red mud, and I was actually encouraged to paddle in the clear water of the stream to wash the mud off. All Dad had to do was to dry me off once back at the bungalow. We were both met with a delicious smell of eggs, bacon, mushrooms tomatoes and sausages. Then, to my amazement, they followed it with toast and marmalade. I shall have to send them to Rosemary Conley classes when we get back home!

To check out the surrounding area, we drove to the village rather than walked because the narrow lanes were too dangerous. We found 'The White Horse' pub and the local store. The natives were so friendly and the pub confirmed that I could go in. There was even a sign saying 'Well-behaved dogs are welcome, children who misbehave should be left outside'.

After lunch, Dad and I showed Mum the walk to Stogumber Railway Station. It was a very pretty station, lots of flowers and benches outside and a picnic area. The picnic area was spoilt by a large notice: NO DOGS! Guess what, they were eating again; cakes and cups of tea which the station mistress had made. I wasn't even offered a crumb. There were a lot of train buffs excitedly waiting for the next steam train to pass through. I really couldn't understand what all the fuss was about, listening to the screaming whistle and lots of smoke belching out the engine as it passed through. It started to drizzle with rain, so the decision was made to return to our holiday home and we made it back just as it started to pour down. We were glad we had changed our minds to walk in the Quantocks. The heavy rain continued all day Sunday and, apart from comfort breaks for me, we stayed in our cosy abode, me snoozing, Dad watching television and Mum reading.

We awoke on Monday to a sunny day and drove to Bicknoller Hill, part of the Quantocks. Mum and Dad puffed their way up, stopping several times to get their breath back noting, on the way there was a poor sheep dying. We then took a level path, me finding fascinating smells on the way amongst the bracken, but Dad kept calling me back as he was worried I might pick up ticks. (I did have my Frontline on!) We took the next path down which was extremely steep. I ran on ahead but it took my two-legs ages, complaining it was hurting their knees. Of course it wasn't a problem for me. Once down, we reported the dying sheep but was asked what colour was its bottom, red or blue? This apparently denotes which farmer it belonged to. We felt very unhelpful as we didn't know.

We drove to a pub for lunch and they both struggled to get out of the car because their knees were aching so much. They agreed this was the last time they would go hill walking. Once refreshed, we drove to Kilve and walked along the coastal path making for St. Audrie's Bay, but had to return as the path had fallen into the sea. We could have got there but it meant walking along the road. However, one of my (clean) poo bags was used to pick huge blackberries. Back at Kilve, we met up with a class of nine to ten year olds who were on holiday too and excitedly showed us the fossils they had found. I got lots of cuddles and pats. Meeting the children encouraged Mum and Dad to clamber over the precarious rocks and stones. We had difficulty keeping our balance, even I found it hard with four legs! Tired, I settled down amongst the stones, having a rest whilst they hunted about. Mum found one fossil but after an hour or so they gave up and we walked to a 13th century chantry which was shored up. The ruin was hopefully waiting for a grant from National Heritage to restore it. Mum and Dad had cream and jam scones and tea (they are always eating) whilst I kept an eye on three cats that were prowling about the garden.

Arriving back, Mum was allowed to pick some apples in the orchard, which complemented the blackberries – not my idea of something special to eat, but they enjoyed them.

We awoke on Tuesday to a dry day. It was Mum's turn to walk me, though I wasn't taken far as a flat walk had been planned later that morning, because rain was expected in the afternoon. Returning, we found Dad hadn't got breakfast and he was grimly hanging onto his walking stick. He said that his right knee had given way after getting out of the shower (the frogs on the shower curtain were still laughing, which I thought was most unkind) and he had fallen over four times!

Mum, unconcerned, sent him down to the village to get the paper whilst she got the breakfast. Dad came back saying the newspaper shop owner thought he was drunk, he had fallen against the counter going in and fell against it again when coming out! Breakfast over, I could tell Mum had got her serious thinking cap on. After a long silence she started speaking. I could hardly believe my ears and I sat my head tilted on one side, then the other side, you know what I mean when us Beardies are listening intently. She said, "Right, I am taking you home. While the dinner is cooking, I'll pack everything up."

By this time, it was pouring with rain and I got shouted at as I was following Mum in and out as she rapidly packed the car! She never shouts, maybe she was a bit stressed. Common sense prevailed at last and I was put in the back on top of the badly loaded boot area, not carefully like Dad had done when we left for our holiday. Never mind, I found it quite comfortable.

The journey back was alright; we even passed one of the steam trains on a lorry being taken back to its base. Mum drove all the way home in torrential rain with Dad hanging on to his seat, complaining she was driving too fast. Four hours later, we arrived at the A & E Department, at Wycombe Hospital, and I watched as Dad hobbled into the unit still hanging on to his walking stick. Leaving Dad there, we drove home, still in the pouring rain. Nanny's partner Jack came round to help us unload. I got shouted at again for getting in their way, so I huffily flounced into my bed; I was only trying to help.

Just over an hour later the phone rang and we drove to collect Dad, this time he was on crutches. The X-ray confirmed he has a seriously arthritic knee and the radiographer could not believe he had just returned from a walking holiday. After visiting his own vet – sorry, doctor – a letter had been sent to a consultant with a view to Dad having an operation. In the meantime Mum is doing all the chores and I am giving Dad extra cuddles in the hope it will help him to recover soon. Considering it was my holiday that was curtailed, he is extremely lucky that I have forgiven him.

JUST KEEPING DAD COMPANY

Joyce Ives

MY STRAWBERRY TEA DAY 2009

The weather forecast was good for the day
I was brushed up as a Beardie should be ready to play.
The journey took us an hour and a half
Arriving there the sight made me laugh.
Beardies bouncing everywhere
Charging around greeting friends who were there:
Black, slate, brown and some fair.
Puppies, youngsters and veterans too
And lots of Beardies going to the loo!

A lady with a booming voice was heard to say,
"Come and join us in all our games today."
It started with Beardies and owners doing musical sits,
One owner playing nearly did the splits.
Then came 'The Puppy Walk – up to twelve months'
Eleven years ago, I was a puppy once.

It was baking hot, we needed cooling
The next game was wet
A pool full of water had us drooling.
One at a time Beardies ran to retrieve their toy
Screeching to a stop, their bums in the air
"What? No way – I'm not going in there!"
Mums and Dads tried to do better
They just succeeded in getting themselves wetter.

The games then stopped, it was time for tea
Mum and Dad, bless them, left nothing for me.

Hearing stories of rescued Beardies who had been sad
Knowing that they now had lovely new owners made me glad.
I watched with amusement at all the antics
Of Beardies trying to win 'The Waggiest Tail'
So many tried but were doomed to fail.

Next came 'Beardie Skittles' which was fun
But before we knew it the day was done.
Flagging Beardies packed into cars,
Children clutching rosettes pleased their pets are stars.

Not long now Beardies – just remember
It is 'The Tramps Tuck-In' in September!

Observed by: SOLEI IVES

Joyce Ives

AN ONGOING SAGA IN SOLEI IVES' HOUSEHOLD

July 2009 passed without mishap apart from me continually visiting my vet as I had gynae problems, but it was being controlled with antibiotics.

August arrived, and my name kept cropping up in numerous discussions. Maybe we are going on my walking holiday after all! Only one suitcase was brought down from the loft and Mum and Dad's clothes were packed and the case snapped shut. A big bag of my towels, my quilt and my food were packed and I was taken round to Nanny and Jack's bungalow. Nothing different there, I am always keeping them company, but I was a bit mystified that all my belongings, including my raincoat, was left in the hall. I charged out into their garden as usual, making sure there were no cats, as they are always leaving their unwanted 'calling cards' and are unwelcome in their garden.

Adele, Mum and Dad's daughter arrived after my lunch, packed all my gear in her car and then took me for a walk round our local common. I was a bit unsure that Adele was supposed to be walking me and I kept looking back to see if my Mum and Dad were joining us. Unfortunately they were nowhere to be seen. We then drove to Reading, arriving at a school and a church which was a very big old building. To my surprise, there were several people with large cameras and others shining huge lighting at some people. A girl shouted 'action' and to my amazement there was someone I recognized: it was Lewis, Mum and Dad's youngest grandson acting the main part in a film. They stopped for a break, so I had a good walk around the film set and the director and producer gave me lots of cuddles; the film crew loved me too! Adele stayed to chaperone Lewis, and Lewis's dad, Dave, took me back to the car. I expected to be taken home, but we arrived back at their house. All my belongings were carried in and I took myself off to explore their house. I looked upstairs and then downstairs, no Mum, Dad or Connor, Lewis's eldest brother, just me and Dave. Oh good, Dave gave me my tea, after all the excitement I was ravenous. It didn't take me long to polish my dish to make it shine. As I have an underactive thyroid gland I am given medication every twelve hours and Mum, bless her heart, hides them in a small amount of sardines so they slide down – delicious! Hey, I like it here, Dave gave me the whole tin of sardines with my pills! Adele and Lewis arrived home and I listened as Dave proudly told them how he had coped looking after me and telling how eager I was taking my pills with the contents of a whole tin of sardines. Everybody laughed at Dave's mistake except me. Shame, it was back to normal after that!

I sat down beside Lewis feeling a bit lost, and he gently hugged me whilst he explained that Mum, Dad, Connor and Connor's friend Milesh had gone to Butlin's. Lewis was supposed to be with them but the filming had been delayed by bad weather, so it wasn't possible for him to go. He wasn't sad as he was enjoying being an actor and he got to see me as well. It was getting dark, and my new carers went up to bed. My bed was downstairs, but it was my turn to look after them so I quietly followed, making sure Lewis was tucked in safely. I crept into Adele and Dave's bedroom and slept beside their bed. I hope they don't tell Dad when he gets back. Saturday morning dawned and I was praised for not disturbing them. I downed my pills (with only a little sardine) as well as my breakfast. Adele took me for a walk through Downley Woods as far as

Naphill and back. It took two hours, Mum only walks me for an hour, so maybe I can stay a bit longer enjoying myself here. Adele left with Lewis to do some more filming whilst I followed Dave around doing his chores. After my lunch Dave took me to St. James Park, Downley for a run, but we had to return quickly as the house alarm was ringing. I didn't realise Dave could run as fast as me. We found that one of the doors wasn't properly shut, so I didn't have a chance to show that I am a good guard dog as well.

Life is so hectic here, there isn't a chance to get bored. We drove off to the film set for a 'wrap party' at the National Film and TV Studios in Beaconsfield. More attention and cuddles from the film crew. I don't know what a wrap party is, but I do hope I am invited to another one.

It is Sunday and another early morning run through Downley Wood and then on to West Wycombe. It was very hilly and Adele kept up with me, not like Mum and Dad dragging behind.

I scattered forty to fifty partridges waddling along encouraging them to take to the air, thank goodness the farmer was still in bed! Sunday came and went as quickly as Friday and

Saturday, Monday was busy too. Adele left for work in the evening and I had Dave and Lewis to look after me. Their doorbell rang and my guarding bark changed to joyous elation.

Mum, Dad and Connor had arrived home, everybody was talking at once and I was beside myself, so happy that we were all back together again.

In mid August my gynae problems had returned and Mum asked to see a specialist. I had an operation to cut back scar tissue which was causing me so much pain. My operation was a success, much to Mum and Dad's relief.

I was right when I told you that there wouldn't be a walking holiday in 2009. I stayed with my Beardie friends whilst Mum and Dad took a sunshine and sea holiday. November arrived and Dad was scheduled for his knee operation. After spending nine hours waiting in his gown, he was told his operation was cancelled due to the anaesthetist's assistant not turning up.

Dad finally had his operation in December; he stayed in hospital for nine days, and we were so pleased to have him home again. Things seem to be going along okay but I hear Dad saying some unusual words while he does his exercises.

Talking about operations, I had to have another one. I had a wart growing right on the edge of my eyelid making my eye very sore, causing an infection. My vet thought it might be cancerous but thankfully it wasn't. Having two anaesthetics in one year, I shed my undercoat and was quite upset to be looking so scruffy, but hopefully by the time you see me again my coat will be looking better.

I wonder what 2010 will bring?

TRIALS AND TRIBULATIONS

It is still 2009, and I continue the saga of life living with my wrinklies.

Dad went into hospital mid December for a complete knee operation, being told the stay would only be three days. The day of the operation was quite traumatic, arriving at reception by 7.30am. Mum said she would walk me once she had seen Dad into the theatre as he was first on his surgeon's list. I settled down in the car knowing she would be back soon. Time passed; I was feeling I really needed a wee, then thank goodness Mum arrived leaping into the car apologising profusely at 9.00am!

After walking me again at lunchtime, Mum kept ringing the hospital to see how Dad was and whether she could visit. On the fourth time of phoning at 3.30pm, she was told not to worry as the nurses on the ward would have been told if there were any problems and they would ring us once Dad was back. Mum left for the hospital at 5.00pm frustrated that no-one had rung her. This is what happened:

1. Dad went into theatre at 10.00am. On opening up his knee, they found they hadn't got the correct sized part.

2. Time was spent ringing around the various hospitals to find one.

3. Right part found at a hospital in Great Missenden.

4. Part is sent by taxi to Wycombe Hospital.

5. Dad arrived back on his ward at 4.00pm swaddled head to toe in foil and blankets, he was almost hypothermic being so long in a cold theatre. (Theatres are kept very cold hoping to stop bugs and bacteria.)

The next three days he kept complaining his knee hurt and the painkillers were stepped up. He still complained, and not being able to administer any more drugs, they took off the bandages to find his skin covered in water blisters (he was allergic to the dressing). On the fourth day he was covered in a very itchy rash and weals diagnosed as erticaeria (nettle rash) a couple of days later, so he wasn't allowed home until the seventh day.

Poor Dad was constantly sick the whole time he was there. The sickness and rash stopped as soon as he got home. I managed to glean the above information listening to Mum talking to people on the telephone and out on my walks.

During this time Mum tried to keep me to my routine which wasn't easy and she often found me following her around looking up at her getting eye contact and being told, "Yes, Solei, I have to do this or that before we can go out." Dad was still quite poorly and needed lots of tender loving care. I found it quite comical watching him doing his exercises and sat at a distance to keep well out of his way.

We spent a lovely Christmas Day with all our family, I was right in amongst all the wrapping paper and there were presents for me too! As the day progressed, Dad needed to lie down and spread himself right along the settee and the former occupants sat on the floor with me. I was lovely and cosy, enjoying all the attention. I had a very cramped journey home amongst all the bulky presents and Dad's crutches, there wasn't even room to lie down!

In February, Mum and Dad had a tea party here inviting everyone who lives in our close to introduce our new next door neighbour. It wasn't a large party as there are only six bungalows. I, of course was the centre of attention and happily greeted our neighbours as they arrived. Eyeing all the delicious snacks, it was difficult to keep my twitching nose away from the low coffee table. It all went so well. Mum is thinking of making it an annual event.

I spent a couple of weeks in April with my Beardie friends whilst the wrinklies had a sunshine and sea holiday. Nothing to report there, apart from enjoying the different walks and having canine company.

May arrived along with Spring Frolic Day. It was really hot and sunny without a puff of wind. Mum entered me in the Primary and Character Working Test and guess what, I passed with 100% and have a Diploma proudly displayed above my bed! We also entered 'Veteran' and I won the second class, what a great day out. I really enjoyed flirting with a beautiful brown Beardie called Harry. He was so handsome and I was quite sad to be told that it was time to go home.

ISN'T IT TIME WE WENT OUT FOR A WALK?

I am getting the feeling that I will not be having a walking holiday this year due to Dad's operated knee and the possibility he may have his other knee done soon. As you can see from the above, not much has happened in my life, because Dad has hogged the limelight and he may do it again next year. I apologise for not being able to report on canine capers instead of human ones.

Christmas is not far away now, here is hoping we all get lots of presents and treats.

DIARY ENTRY 2010

I am finding it quite a trial living with my guardians, Joyce and John to you, Mum and Dad to me. Our lives continue to lurch from one drama to another. It is a wonder the RSPCA haven't investigated them as several times I have had to stand right in front of my Mum, wagging my tail furiously, jumping up and down to attract her attention to remind her she hasn't fed me.

At the beginning of this year, because of Dad's second new replacement knee, Mum had the pleasure of walking me. I find her so embarrassing, she is always falling over. I hear a thud, look round and there she is flat on her back, rubbing her head. Okay, we were going down an icy slope in the woods at the time, but I had no trouble at all. Maybe it is because I have four legs.

A couple of weeks later, we had ten inches of snow (Mum measured it). Early morning we were wading through the cold stuff and because the kerbs were nowhere to be seen, over she goes again, falling on her side into the road. I looked around and it was lucky no one saw her and no cars were about to run her over.

A week after that we were out in the garden. Mum feeds the birds every morning before she walks me and I follow her about expectantly, ready for the off. Mum took longer as she was clearing the paths of snow, and unbelievably she trips up a step, and crash she was down again, face first, banging both her knees. The pot of bird seed flew up in the air and scattered everywhere. I have never seen the birds so happy!

At the end of January my best friend Kiri came to stay for two whole weeks. Thank goodness there are now two of us to look after Mum, it is such a huge responsibility for me on my own! After keeping us awake the first two nights, pacing up and down, whining, Kiri soon settled down to our routine. We had lovely walks and raced off together chasing deer and foxes, Kiri returning first to check that Mum was still standing upright! The days flew by with nothing untoward happening until four days before Kiri was due to go home. Every evening Mum walks us to the bottom of our close for our late night wee. I am always off the lead and I squat as quickly as I can on the grass and then race back for my supper. This particular night, Kiri was on the lead and I spied through the blackness (there is no street lighting) another dog across the road. Well, no one is allowed to walk their dog the same time as me, so I barked constantly telling them that this was my territory. Mum shouted at me, calling me back, but I needed to protect Kiri as she was in season. With me making such a noise, Mum shouting too, the commotion set Kiri off into a frantic bouncing mode and somehow she got between Mum's legs and Mum fell backwards into the road, banging her head again.

After an awful cracking sound, everything went quiet for a while, Mum was still holding Kiri's lead lying in the road moaning. The owner of the dog I was barking at came across, took Kiri whilst Mum rolled over getting to her feet. She had embarrassed me again! Funnily enough I knew the dog I had challenged as I had often walked with her. Mum staggered back home with us obediently by her side, telling Dad when we got in that the back of her head really hurt and was swelling rapidly into the shape of half an orange. Dad immediately consulted an emergency doctor as she had a head injury. We were quickly shoved into the back of the car to drive to A & E, Wycombe Hospital. Five hours later we stirred as they both got back into the car and returned home. It was 2.00am before we all finally went to bed. Kiri and I chatted for a while and we both came to the conclusion that my Mum needs to be rehomed as we cannot cope with her. Kiri happily left us a couple of days later, thankful to leave the responsibility of Mum in my safe paws.

It was now back to our normal routine and every morning I tour the garden checking out who has had the audacity to enter into my territory. Normally I only find feline odour around but on this particular morning the scent was far stronger: foxes. How dare they! Big holes had been dug under our fences which Dad later blocked off, only to find they were then jumping the fences. They got bolder and even trotted through the garden during the day checking first that I was indoors. Mum and Dad noted that they had superb coats and couldn't believe they roamed through our estate. We found out later that one of the neighbours fed them a can of dog meat every day. Weeks went by until one morning Mum and I were shocked to see that one of the foxes had started digging a hole under the shed. Dad was summoned, and he quickly shovelled all the soil back treading it down. My eyes nearly popped out of my head, he stood and peed all over the disturbed earth. Apparently he had read somewhere that foxes do not like human male urine! "That will stop them," he said. It didn't, as two days later I walked up to the conservatory door to tell them that the foxes had succeeded in gaining access under the shed again. I knew it was now ready for her to have her cubs. Mum and Dad took one look at me, the whole of my head, beard and paws were covered in muddy soil where I had been investigating their den. This I regretted, as it was the bath tub for me. Great activity ensued: Mum and Dad worked together filling in the hole, boarded all along the side of the shed, big wooden pegs banged into the ground and then mixed up some powder into a watering can, pouring around the area. The packet showed a picture of a deer, a fox and a rabbit. I haven't seen a deer or a rabbit in the garden. The foxes still walk through our garden, but they haven't attempted to dig under the shed again. One afternoon, Mrs. Fox was happily sitting in the middle of my lawn and then started scratching furiously. This occurrence sent Mum straight to our vets to

Beardies World

pick up some Frontline as the last thing I need is fleas jumping into my coat, or, even worse sarcoptic mange!

I don't know whether you all realise, but I am twelve years old, and I am losing my hearing. When Mum or Dad call me, they end up standing in front of me calling my name in a much louder voice. They are also using 'signing' when they get my attention and want me to go with them. Apparently they used this method with Kizzy, their first Beardie, when she went deaf, and it worked well with her. It was easier then because they used to send Emma and Muffin (their second and third Beardies) to go and find her and bring her to them. Now, as I am the only one, they have to go and fetch me themselves. Still, I must admit it is good exercise for them.

There has been no mention of my walking holiday which is usually a week at the end of September or early October, because Dad is having trouble with his first replacement knee and is waiting for a scan as the hospital doctor thinks it might have come loose and that is why he is having so much pain with it. If it means another operation, then my holiday will be cancelled again, but so will Mum and Dad's, so sad faces all round.

2010 – LIFE ON HOLD

How time has flown by. I had begun to get fidgety, and to be honest, I didn't know whether to share my thoughts with you this time as bad things still keep following us around. Anyway here goes!

Dad saw his knee specialist and the man decided that Dad should have extra physiotherapy on both his knees and then see him again in September.

Although it was getting late in the year, I found myself listening to 'the olds' sitting on the settee together (they always do this when there is something to discuss). They were moaning that they only had one week's holiday this year and Mum was emphasizing that I hadn't had my walking holiday for two years and if I wasn't taken away it would be three years! Now this sounded interesting. I stretched and yawned, bum up in the air, my tail wagging. I pushed in between them and rested my head on their laps, giving them my melancholy eyes stare, looking from one to the other.

Dad said it was too late in the year to go away because of inclement weather in November, but Mum persevered, saying once I had my main walks each day, which are not so long now as I am nearly thirteen, we could then cosy up indoors in the warm, just relaxing, reading books and magazines, and me dozing in my bed.

Hurrah, bouncing Beardies, they have booked to take me to Swanage staying in a bungalow for a week! Good old Mum, she usually gets her own way. The 8th November arrived and the dogmobile was packed and I excitedly jumped in ready for a new adventure. It gets pretty boring in your own back yard, don't you agree? We stopped for lunch at Sandford, just outside Wareham; Dad checked the pub accepted canines, which was a yes.

We were allowed the key to our bungalow at 3.00pm and shown around our holiday home by a young lady. She switched on the central heating and it soon warmed up. She then left wishing us a happy holiday. Dad set up my grooming table in the garage whilst Mum unpacked the suitcases and boxes. The bungalow was beautiful with a lovely garden surrounding it. Once everything was to Mum and Dad's satisfaction, we went and explored. In less than ten minutes walking through the narrow roadways with pretty and quirky bungalows either side, we reached the cliff tops and looked down to the beach and the sea. There were lots of steps down to reach the beach, but as it was getting dusk, we returned to the bungalow. Mum drew the curtains, making it lovely and cosy, and I stretched out full-length dozing while Mum and Dad, smiling and relaxed, ate cake and drank cups of tea. I let out a happy grunt and fell asleep. We were on holiday at last.

I opened one eye as Mum answered her mobile phone. I was half awake anyway as it was nearly my tea time. Mum listened, phone clamped to her ear, then switching it off, she said to Dad: "You are not going to believe this." A voice at the other end of her phone told her Nanny, aged 94, who now lives in a nursing home, had had a fall, hitting the back of her head on a coffee table. Jack, her partner who was visiting, rushed to get somebody to help as she had become unconscious. The ambulance men had been called and she was taken to hospital. Needless to say, the rest of the evening was not at all relaxing, due to phone calls to Adele, their daughter, and receiving three calls from the doctor in A & E, requesting information on Nanny's demeanour. They said they would be keeping Nanny in overnight under observation and would be doing various tests and scans.

We went to bed quite early, but as usual, Mum was up at 7.00am to give me my medication and breakfast. Usually on holidays, Mum then goes back to bed for a while, but I was surprised to see Dad get up, shower and dress. He and I both togged up in our waterproofs as it was blowing a gale with torrential rain. We were not out long as the weather was so abysmal; I was looking forward to getting back and dried. After their breakfast, we could cosy up as planned: great. WRONG! I was totally confused to see Mum packing up the boxes and repacking the suitcases. They had decided we couldn't enjoy the holiday knowing Nanny was very unwell, especially as her doctor again expressed his concern. I was absolutely devastated. I had been so looking forward to my holiday, but Nanny comes first because we love her and she feeds me biscuits every time I visit her! Breakfast finished, everything was piled in the porch and Dad managed to back the dogmobile as near to the door as possible to load up. It wasn't very long before we set out for home, driving through rivers of water running down the roads.

Fortunately, it had stopped raining by the time we unloaded the car (we heard later on the news that Swanage had flooded in places).

A quick lunch, a quick walk for me and then we were driving to Slough to visit Nanny in hospital. Mum's mobile rang;

it was Adele telling us to go straight to Nanny's nursing home as she had just been discharged and was on her way back. Adele would meet us at the home. We three arrived at the home and sat and waited for her to return. Over half an hour went by and then Adele walked in. I was very pleased to see her, but, ignoring me at first, she demanded to know where Nanny was. We were later informed that the ambulance driver had aborted the journey as Nanny was unwell and she didn't have an assistant on board to help look after her. I looked at each of them one by one, and it seemed that the plans were about to be changed again. They were talking rapidly and I heard my name mentioned. Adele was to take me home with her. What an eventful day. I was expecting to be picked up before 5.00pm, my tea time.

Mum, Dad and Jack eventually picked me up just after ten o'clock. Adele had made me some scrambled egg for my tea but I wouldn't eat it, so I was quite hungry, though she did walk me. On the way home Mum's mobile rang again, it was the hospital saying a two man ambulance had at last arrived after Nanny waiting six hours, and she was on her way back to her nursing home. The staff there eventually got her into bed at midnight!

So this was the end of my holiday, eighteen hours in total! As my visit was so brief, I am sorry but I am unable to recommend the area of Swanage where we were staying. Perhaps we will try again.

Joyce Ives

2011 – LOOKING FORWARD

I became quite depressed not having my holiday last year, especially as I am a veteran and am not sure how many holidays I will enjoy in the future. It is okay living with my 'olds'; I am quite busy helping them with caring for Jack, Nanny's partner. I still get my morning walk starting about 7.15am. Mum always takes me as Dad walks round to Jack's to help him wash, dress and get his breakfast. What I have noticed is that my walks are not so long now as Mum needs to get back as they are so busy. I go with them during the day, checking on Jack, and Dad gives me a short walk in the afternoon and again in the evening when they put him to bed. Then of course I travel in the dogmobile to visit Nanny, who is ninety-five years old, in her nursing home. I love all the attention I get there. One of the residents enjoys walking me around the lounge on my lead, and of course the main reason I go is for the titbits.

Our lives changed somewhat when Jordan, Mum and Dad's seventeen-year-old grandson, moved in with us for five months. We were even busier than before. I was woken up earlier as Jordan had to leave the bungalow by 8.10am to go to football college, run by the Chelsea Academy. He only had one football strip which had to be washed every night for him to wear the next day. Mum thought it would be easier to get a second set but when Jordan told her the cost the colour drained from her face. This information made her continue washing the strip each evening.

Beardies World

I was given the job of snuffling in Jordan's face every morning to wake him up. His bedroom was quite small and I had to negotiate my way through all his paraphernalia stacked in piles on the floor. Mum found it a nightmare to clean his room. I helped by hoovering up the biscuit crumbs. It never got dusted until he moved out! His friends stayed occasionally at weekends dossing down on the floor because they had a football match the next day. The smell of the eggs, bacon, mushrooms, fried tomatoes, toast and homemade marmalade for breakfast resulted in me lying near my dish, just in case there were any leftovers, but do you know, there was never anything left for me. No wonder their heights ranged from six feet one inch to six feet four inches considering all the food they demolished; Mum looked like a wizened old lady amongst them! We really missed him when he left to live with his Mum again. Of course there was less washing and ironing (we thought only teenage girls changed their clothes every few hours, not boys) and Dad was pleased the food bill had reduced. Jordan calls in occasionally and I always give him a happy greeting bouncing up and down, wagging my tail furiously.

Do you remember me telling you about Lewis, our youngest grandson, who had the main part in a film called *The Confession*? Well, he went to Hollywood for the Oscars. All our family were really excited. I find excitement expressed by humans is really squeaky voices with everyone talking at once and lots of laughter. Although I was at the filming a couple of times, I was only watching, so I wasn't allowed to go.

In March, Mum and Dad needed a break from caring for Jack (he has terminal prostate cancer which has spread to his bones). They took themselves off for five days to a Warner Hotel. I went to stay at my Beardie friend Kiri's house. She was six weeks in whelp and excitedly told me she had quite a few babies in her tummy. We are always taken on lovely walks when I stay there, to the woods and down alongside the local canal.

Kizzy, Mum and Dad's first Beardie, jumped into this canal; she was definitely a water girl, even the smallest muddy puddle got the treatment of being wallowed in. However, I digress. We three, Hannah, Kiri and I were enjoying a great walk, reaching the gate to proceed alongside the canal. Usually their Mum holds Hannah back as we pass through because Hannah whips Kiri up into a frenzy, and me. Otherwise we charge through, barking and bouncing about, not the correct behaviour when we should be thinking of Kiri's condition. On this particular morning their Mum's mind was elsewhere, and we three charged through the gate. Kiri was really on a high, cavorting about, showing off to me that she was no different to us. SHE FELL INTO THE CANAL! Hannah and I looked down at Kiri as she swam, coat spreading out around her, looking for a way up. She was starting to panic getting tired, beginning to sink, heavy with her babies.

We watched in awe as her Mum lay flat on her stomach hanging over the edge with one arm reaching down, the other holding onto the edge trying to grab Kiri's collar, eventually hauling her up and out, both of them of course soaking wet. On dry land, Kiri shook the excess water from her coat, spraying us in the process, charged at us as if it was our fault, then off we ran together as though nothing had happened. Just to let you know, Kiri had eight babies. It will be interesting to hear when they go to their new homes if they love water.

OH HANNAH THIS WAS OUR FAULT!

I have to report to you that the foxes are still coming into my garden, and now unbeknownst to another neighbour, they managed to dig under his shed and have three cubs. This really is a nightmare. One evening, the vixen was carrying one of her cubs and managed to jump over our five foot fence. As the cubs grew, small holes were dug under the fence to let them through as they were too heavy to be heaved over.

On the 12th June every year there is a Village Care Open Gardens Day. Many proud people in the village open up their gardens for the villagers to view and admire. Tickets are bought at the Village Hall, and a map is given showing whose gardens are on show including one of the larger gardens that also serves up tea and cakes.

Well, our garden was going to be one of them to be shown, but Mum had to decline as the cubs have used our garden as a playground and have flattened all her lovely plants, including her much loved Alpine beds! I often lie on the lawn on guard, but when they do appear, they are too quick for me. I just run backwards and forwards huffing and puffing.

Last week, I was feeling a bit uncomfortable, but wasn't sure how to tell Mum. She was sitting in her chair in the snug, reading a paper, so I pushed my head under it moving it out the way to get her attention. She gave me a stroke, re-positioned her paper and carried on reading. On the third attempt she got the message. She started to run her hands gradually over my body. No Mum, not there, no, not there either, no you are getting colder – yes, yes you are getting closer, then I kept perfectly still until her fingers found the spot. "Oh, it's a tick," she said, surprised. Dad came over and I stood like a statue whilst they fussed over me, clearing my fur away from it. Dad, my hero, got it out with tweezers, turning it anticlockwise. Five days later in the early evening I was again chasing out the foxes and nearly caught one of the cubs; Mum noticed that I emerged from the bushes limping on my right paw. She thought I had strained it, but when walking me the next morning I was still limping. Mum scrutinised my paw thoroughly, maybe I had cut a pad or torn one of my claws. To her horror, there was a huge tick, full of my blood that had burrowed up one of my nail beds. This time I screamed. Mum and Dad couldn't get it out, so it was a trip to our vets. Mum and Dad and a nurse held on to me whilst the vet pulled it out. Maybe I had got it off of one of the foxes; Mum had put Frontline on me, but we were told by my vet that the best thing to use for the treatment of troublesome ticks is Advantix.

I am so looking forward to my next holiday, though it's not until the beginning of October. We are off to the Isle of Wight, staying at The Indian Summer House, in the grounds of Osbourne House. This was built a century ago by Queen Victoria for the royal children in a style to conjure up the atmosphere of India. If that is the case, do you think I will have to look out for tigers instead of foxes?

SOLEI

MY TRAVELOGUE FOR 2011

An awful lot has happened since I last made an entry last year telling you that my next holiday wouldn't be until October 2011.

Sadly, Jack who I told you about died in June, and we all miss him. Mum and Dad had to sell Nanny's bungalow which Jack was living in to pay fully for her nursing care fees. Mum and Dad's children helped sorting through everything. I kept well out of the way, sleeping in the garden. They managed to empty it in two weeks as the new owner had already sold her property and wanted to move in as soon as possible.

As we no longer had Jack to look after, Mum sat at her computer trying to find a holiday cottage so we could take an earlier break. I was well pleased when she found a converted barn called 'The Parlour' in Sutton Poyntz, near Weymouth, in Dorset, and it was vacant the second week in August.

As you know, I am well used to the routine of packing up and piling everything in the dogmobile. Mum and I are also well used to hearing Dad moan that everything is pushed and shoved in the wells and on the back seat whilst I lord it in the back with plenty of space! I am a veteran and I must have my comfort.

I loved our accommodation apart from having to go up and down two wooden polished steps leading from the kitchen into the lounge diner. I hated them as I kept slipping, so Mum had to lay my towels across them, which made it easier for me. In the dining area there was a metal spiral staircase leading up to a gallery-style double bedroom. We didn't use this because of Dad's knees, so we used the bedroom off the dining room. This had French doors leading to a small enclosed garden which had picket fencing adjoining the owner's garden next door.

Whilst Mum and Dad unpacked, I explored the garden to find, to my astonishment a clipped Beardie boy, the same age as me, wagging his tail furiously, peering through the fence. He told me his name was Dillon. It was love at first sight. I did hope we might walk together, but his guardians were very busy people.

Later that afternoon, we walked to the beautifully kept village which had a large pond with a stream running through it. I have never seen so many ducks happily swimming about. Many of the cottages backed onto the stream and each had beautiful little bridges for access. Overlooking the pond was the 'Springhead' pub. It used to be a hotel some years ago which frequently accommodated entertainers during the summer season who were appearing in shows at Weymouth. Now it is just a pub with a restaurant and upstairs is used by the owners. Well behaved canines are allowed inside.

We didn't get much sleep the first night. As the floors were wooden, every time I got up to change my position, my claws made a lot of noise as I scrabbled to get up and down. The next day Mum sorted out the problem by laying all the covers and towels from the dogmobile all around the bedroom. Each morning the floor looked quite messy as the towels slid each time I moved about, but it did solve the noise problem.

After breakfast we walked to Bowleaze Cove along the South West Coastal Path. The cliffs had fallen away in places and for a while I was put on a lead for my safety. A new path had been roughly made away from the cliff and it was a very very difficult climb, with steep stepping places. Dad had an awful job pushing Mum up and then me, I had four paws but he still had the job of helping me too. He was so brave as he had to climb up all by himself with a heavy knapsack on his back. I was in a fearful funk that he wouldn't make it!

We were aiming for Osmington Mills, but seeing a sign for Osmington and a pub called 'The Sunray', which was only a quarter of a mile away, we abandoned going there because it was one-and-a-quarter miles further on and we still had the journey home to consider. We arrived at 'The Sunray' hot and tired and I crashed out in the shade of the pub garden. Please note that canines were not allowed inside. I refused my lunch until the two-legs put some meaty morsels in my dish.

With the help of the Ordnance Survey map, we returned home by a much prettier route crossing many fields, with a white horse cut out in chalk looking down on us from the hillside. Back at our barn we three went to sleep, giving our aching bones a rest.

The next day we drove to Burning Cliff owned by The National Trust, way above Ringstead Bay. A viewpoint was there with beautiful views. Then we drove down to Ringstead

Bay; parking cost £5.00 but Dad thought it was worth it when you could stay all day as on the site was a gift shop which served hot food and had toilets. We were determined to walk to Osmington Mills and found 'The Smugglers Inn'. It was a very large pub, and please note canines were allowed inside. There was a free car park, a play area for children and the pub also included a special menu for the little two-legs. Mum and Dad demolished coffee and cream buns.

We then moved on to explore taking very steep steps down to a stony, pebbly beach following a stream running into the sea. What with Dad's knees and my age, we decided this beach wasn't suitable and walked back to Ringstead Bay, having a picnic on the way. It was a very hot day again and very windy. On reaching the Bay, we found this too was stony and cobbly but was packed with holiday makers struggling to keep their windbreaks upright to shelter behind them. I paddled for a while then found a comfortable huge smooth rock to lie on to have a rest and watched the children having to chase their escaped beach balls which kept me amused.

Once back at the barn, I lay out on the lawn whilst Mum and Dad drank tea and read their books. It's about time they gave me a rest.

The following day it was raining and after a quick walk I was dried with Mum's hairdryer. Once we three had our breakfast; they sat down and read their books cosily sitting in front of a log fire in the huge fireplace. Dad made it. I didn't know you could have a real fire indoors! After lunch it had stopped raining and we drove back to the Burning Cliff. It was still blowing a gale and we had difficulty keeping upright. We chose one of the footpaths hoping to walk sheltered from the wind, but I was grateful when they turned back to seek refuge in the dogmobile and drove back to the barn.

Our five day holiday passed by all too quickly and once again, we returned home. I always love to get back to check out my familiar area seeking new exciting and interesting smells.

October arrived and we were off again, this time driving onto a very large metal clanging ferry. Canines were allowed on the upper deck, but because I am elderly, they left me in the dogmobile on my own as humans are not allowed in the great big metallic car park. I was really pleased when they came back and we drove down the ramp onto the road. We had arrived on the Isle of Wight.

We were too early to pick up our keys for The Indian Summer House and found a lovely modern pub called 'The Lifeboat' overlooking the estuary full of boats. I am pleased to report that canines are allowed and whilst Mum and Dad ate their fish and chips, plenty of people came over to give me cuddles.

Our cottage was very old and dark used by Queen Victoria's children as a playhouse. The darkness was caused by the wisteria and rambling roses growing around the huge windows. We liked it as it was spacious, warm and comfortable.

After lunch the following day, Dad drove us to Ryde, then onto Sandown. We preferred Sandown, being very sandy, and I was allowed on the beach as it was October, and we decided we would return again as we found a pub that allowed canines.

Mum and Dad sorted through brochures and we visited Arreton Old Village, which dated back a thousand years. I plodded around with them, in and out of craft shops, glass blowing, pottery, a fudge shop (I wasn't allowed in there). Mum came out with a big package! There was a huge pub called 'The Dairyman's Daughter' and we had lunch outside. We were sure it could cater for at least two hundred people; the dinner plates were huge and piled with roast beef and all the vegetables. I wasn't surprised when my wrinklies couldn't empty their plates.

Another dawn, another day, we set off to walk down to the Solent. We were told it was quite a long way, but hey, we had plenty of time; we were on holiday after all. It was downhill all the way and arriving (eventually) we watched young children learning how to sail dinghies. Some were getting caught up in the sails when they lowered them as it was extremely windy and instructors in ribs (rubber inflatable boats) were roaring to their aid. As I was getting bored, we walked along the walled coastline as far as we could go as our Ordnance Survey map showed a castle there. We reached the castle grounds' wall, then climbed up beside the wall which was hard going, finally reaching a locked gate. Disappointed, we had to turn round and negotiate the steep descent. The ground was littered with acorns. Yes, you guessed it, Mum's walking boots turned into roller skates and she sat down on her bottom with a thump. I watched in amusement as Dad clinging to a tree tried to manhandle her to her feet. "I told you to be careful," he said. It took us quite a long time walking back uphill to our Summer House.

As I had spent most of my time on the lead, I was taken to Parkhurst Forest. It was next door to Parkhurst and Albany Prison. It is a huge wood with lots of wide and narrower paths running through it. We were told to look for red squirrels, but didn't see even one and never saw any escaped prisoners either. I really enjoyed myself, meeting lots of people walking their canine companions. From there we drove to Yarmouth, just a small complex of shops. We settled for 'The Bugle Coaching Inn'. Once again, I was allowed to enter and the meal they had there was very good as I heard them scraping their plates!

We then drove to the Old Battery and the Needles car park. We had to pay even though Dad showed his disabled badge. The climb up was very steep, it was blowing an absolute gale and gusting; we made sure we were away from the cliff edges as it was quite frightening, I really didn't like it. At the top, we found disabled parking bays! The man down at the car park didn't tell us this as he was after Dad's money.

Mum and Dad were quite interested in the history there. I must admit I was bored and couldn't wait to get back to the car park.

Joyce Ives

HAVING A REST

Wednesday was cold and drizzly and we visited a lovely village called Godshill. The pavements were very narrow and the place was heaving with two-legs. They had a large model village there which we shuffled round and I had to walk to heel, but my day was brightened when we visited a tea shop that had very large immaculate gardens separated out into different themes. There were two tame chickens walking around, picking up crumbs people had thrown for them. Mum and Dad could see I was fed up, so we left and drove to St. Catherine's Point where they had lunch at 'The Buddle Inn'. Not once on the Isle of Wight was I refused access – the island is very canine friendly. The rest of the afternoon was spent walking in Brighstone Forest where we met a very sweet Beardie crossed with a border collie. She looked like a puppy but she informed me she was nine years old.

We awoke on Thursday morning to the sound of a ship blowing its horn, looking out, we could see it was really foggy. It had cleared by the time we had breakfast and it turned out to be sunny and no wind. Mum and Dad decided this day was to be a rest day (they are getting old you know) so they did a bit of packing and then had lunch in the garden.

They sat in the sun reading their books, I was grateful for the rest and snoozed in the shade. Our garden was half an acre of lawns with a mini woodland as well, so I loved to go off and have a potter by myself.

Finally, we celebrated New Year's Day 2012 at our local pub. I like going there because practically everyone knows me and comes over to say hello and give me a cuddle. It was a special day as male Morris Dancers and female Morris Dancers jingled and stick-banged their way through lots of dances in the car park. I couldn't hear most of the music as I am pretty deaf, but I did watch with interest at the men banging their drums and the tuba being played. What a strange instrument, I haven't seen one of those before.

Another New Year to look forward to, I just hope it will be a good one.

Joyce Ives

STOPPING FOR A BREAK

CATCH-UP TIME 2012

Did you Beardies enjoy the snow? When I was younger I loved it, I ate it, rolled in it and had a wonderful time. However, this year, I preferred to look out through the windows, watching Mum and Dad with our neighbours struggling to clear the driveway and our cul-de-sac. I snuggled up in my duvet; being older now, I am also wiser!

RETURNING FROM MY WALK

I haven't been so well these last few months and have been visiting my vet, who is always happy to see us knowing that my folks' credit card will be produced at the end of our consultation.

Last November, I suffered a fit and was rushed to the vets. Our vet wasn't on duty so another man took my blood. The results, he said, were normal apart from my liver function, which was raised. He gave me some pills to keep me calm and so far I haven't had any more fits.

In January, I was feeling worse, didn't want my meals and if I did eat, I was occasionally sick. I went on my usual walks, but not so far, and my tummy was a bit upset. Another visit to our vet, I was due my six-monthly thyroid check and Mum told him I wasn't feeling well. After checking my notes, he saw the raised liver function. My blood was sent off for the thyroid and also another liver check. He also asked for a poo sample. Oh, how gross! I watched with disdain as Mum pushed bits of my poo into a plastic tube.

My blood results showed that my thyroid levels were double what they should be and we were to halve my tablets, and my liver function was very high too. A month's supply of medication to help my liver was being put out for collection. I noticed when Dad returned to the car after collecting them he was white as a sheet; my pills to help my liver cost £97.53! A few more days later, my vet rang again and told us I had campylobacter and I needed strong antibiotics. No wonder I was feeling so poorly. I had stopped eating and drinking and Mum was trying so many things to whet my appetite, but to no avail. I didn't even want to go for a walk. On the third evening, I was so weak, I wobbled along on the point of collapse. When we went to bed, I chose the vet bed to lie on at the bottom of Mum's bed. There is also one between their beds which I also use. (The olds have separate beds as Dad is a very restless sleeper and used to hog the duvet cover, leaving Mum awake and cold.)

During the night I awoke to find that Mum's bed was shaking all the time, so I moved round to check on her to find that she was sobbing. I could smell the salty wetness on her pillow.

The faint light of the clock showed that Dad was fast asleep, mouth wide open snoring, even I could hear it so it must have been loud as you know I am quite deaf. He had no idea that Mum was so stressed. I was so tired and feeble and her crying went on for such a long time. I lay down between their beds looking from one to the other. I wasn't sure if I was going to get better. I loved them so much and I knew they loved me too.

When morning arrived, I dragged myself to my daytime duvet and lay there watching a puffy, red-eyed Mum in the kitchen starting to get breakfast. She came and knelt in front of me holding my bowl. Each time she offered the bowl I turned my head away. "No, I couldn't possibly eat that!" We stared at each other, neither giving way. Again and again she tried, finally she put her fingers in my bowl and scooped up some creamy looking pudding. "Haven't I told you, I don't want anything!" I watched the salty liquid run down her cheeks again and was shocked when she rammed her fingers coated with the claggy stuff into my mouth. Yuk, or maybe it is not so bad? She offered more and I licked it off her fingers until I finally helped myself from the bowl. Oh, she is smiling and she is pleased. I lay still, quietly watching her. Another bowl was put in front of me, a warm, watered-down milky liquid. I polished this off too. This was the turning point and I gradually got my appetite back, I heard over and over again Mum telling her friends that porridge was the answer to my recovery.

Four weeks went by and another blood test revealed that my thyroid levels had improved, but my liver function only slightly. Another blood test has to be taken in another six weeks. I am feeling a lot better, but Mum and Dad have reduced the length of my walks.

I enjoy just lying on the lawn when dry, and wait for the red kites to come down to pick up the pieces of fat put out for them (I hate fat). Usually just one swoops down picking up the fat in its claws and flies up over the top of my head. They are so beautiful. Only when several swoop down at different angles, I move indoors; their huge flapping wings are too much for me to tolerate! Dad has sat patiently with the camera to snap the birds with me lying on the lawn watching them come down, but they are too quick for the camera shutter and he gets so frustrated. He would like a more sophisticated camera but he can't afford a new one AND my vet bills!

Another monthly visit to my vet for my thyroid levels and liver function revealed my thyroid levels needed halving again and my liver function was sort of alright. I am feeling a lot better and Mum and Dad have increased my walks again.

In April, Easter Sunday, we three drove to Thame as there was a big show being held there. The weather forecast wasn't very good, but we were very lucky with the weather, hardly any rain. I was a bit bored, wandering in and out of all the stands; there were so many selling clothes, others, ornaments carved out of wood, too many to mention. Delicious smells wafted across my nose and I watched with interest as Dad queued for snacks and drinks. In the main arena, there was carriage racing with horses trying to beat each other for the fastest time around the obstacles. Huge shire horses plodded around the arena dressed in beautiful livery. Then we watched motor bikes whizzing through the air over ten people lying in the grass. I was grateful Mum and Dad refused for us to go and join them!

As you know, it was also the Spring Frolic in April and the weather was awful; it rained practically the whole time, but do you know there were still lots of owners of my Beardie friends enjoying the day, though many of the games were played in the Village Hall! Oh and yes, my nose told me that everyone was enjoying the lovely spread of food, and as for the cakes, what can I say? I wasn't offered a crumb!

My next blood test revealed that my thyroid level was spot on, but my liver level had climbed again even though I was taking medication to keep me well. I looked up at Mum and Dad's face and they looked troubled, but hey, don't worry guys, it's my fourteenth birthday on the 4th May and we can enjoy my day.

Goodness gracious! Summer has come and people are walking about in shorts. I was driven to the woods where it was cool,

Beardies World

the sun being shaded by the leaves. I really do not like the hot weather and was grateful to just wander along at my own pace.

The 20th May was Nanny's 96th birthday, and we travelled over to her home with a cake and lots of presents. The carers had set the tables for her birthday tea and just before the residents arrived at the tables, Mum scooped me up and sat me on a clean towel placed on a chair next to Nanny. She smiled and gave me a hug and then I was down on the floor again as quick as you like before the nurse came in. I was shocked: I have never sat up at a table before!

A couple of days later, I spent time with my best friends, Auntie Barbara and Uncle Michael, whilst Mum and Dad went on a jaunt to Oxford by coach. I enjoyed the change of venue but wasn't up to eating my dinner. Their grandchildren were laughing at me as I tried in vain to bury my dish pushing it around the kitchen. The following afternoon we took a trip to Aylesbury as Mum and Dad had a meeting at the Head Office of the Trust that cares for Nanny. It was another hot day, but walking into the building it was lovely and cool, the meeting was nearly two hours and as usual Mum and Dad were congratulated for having such a well behaved Beardie.

At 2.00am the next morning, I awoke feeling awful and sicked up my supper. Mum and Dad sorted me out, washed my beard, and settled me down. Mum went back to sleep. Dad heard me blundering about in the hall; I was feeling sick again, it must be the very humid night. We went out into the garden and Dad sat on the bench in his pyjamas. Oh dear, this is a nightmare, I can hardly stand. The next thing I knew I was being lifted onto my cot by Mum and Dad and they tried to make me comfortable by bolstering my back, neck and head with bedding. Mum, in her nightie, sat on a foot stool really close to me and worked her fingers gently through my coat with tiny circular movements which really helped me. It was just before dawn and the birds were beginning to stir; the dew came down and the temperature dropped; I was covered up and Mum and Dad went separately to put on their dressing gowns so I wasn't left alone. I couldn't lift my head but just followed them with my eyes. A little later, they took it in turns getting dressed and again we three were together. I always love it whenever we are together. It make us a family. I wasn't at all bothered when I saw my vet walk towards me with his nurse carrying a case. The wind was blowing softly, wafting the scents of lilac and azalea around us. I sighed as my kind vet took all my pain away. Mum and Dad, I shall see you both when we meet over the Rainbow Bridge, I will be waiting for you …

04.05.1998–24.05.2012

A BEARDIE LAMENT

Don't ever buy a hairy dog!
I speak as one who knows,
'Cos a pretty, fluffy puppy
Gets more hairy as it grows.
You'll fight a losing battle
As you grapple with the hairs,
You'll find them on the carpet
Down the drain and on the stairs.
And don't expect your family
To understand your plight –
Instead of giving sympathy,
They'll laugh with all their might.
For fourteen years I've battled
And I'm weary as can be,
I've just dipped into my savings
To buy Hoover number three.
But when she slips away from us
I'll know I'll shed a tear
I'll forget the work she's made
Each day, each month, each year.
But then I'll start aworrying,
If some kind Soul up there,
Will carry on where I left off –
To clean up Solei's hair!

REUNITED

… Hello and welcome Solei, yes it's me Muffin, we have been waiting for you. Do you remember Kizzy? Please let me introduce you to Emma, Mum and Dad's second Beardie, she was the first to pass over the Rainbow Bridge, and then Kizzy. I was the next to join them. Now you arriving completes our canine family.

We love it here: no aches and pains, plenty to eat, and the sun shines. Look at the beautiful meadows we play and roll about in, the sparkling river to splash and swim in. Actually Solei, we call it 'Heaven'.

Now you are here, you can share our task of watching the Rainbow Bridge. The Bridge gets quite crowded sometimes and an extra pair of eyes will help us to watch out for Mum and Dad. We will be so pleased to see them. They must be lonely without us.

Now come with us, Solei, and we will show you around. No, you don't need to keep an eye on The Bridge yet; we are pretty sure it will be a while before they come across to join us. In the meantime, why don't we have some fun…?

DOGOGRAPHIES OF KIZZY, EMMA, MUFFIN AND SOLEI

KIZZY was our first slate Beardie and she was an absolute joy, so easy to train and a very friendly biddable girl, although a bit of a 'wimp'; if she ever hurt herself, she would just sit down and not move until the problem was resolved for her.

At thirteen months old she welcomed Emma with open paws and loved her company, introducing her to rivers and streams, and lovely country walks. She was the most mischievous character out of our four Beardies.

When Muffin arrived, Kizzy tolerated her, enjoying the extra company sharing her with Emma. Nothing fazed Kizzy, she was so laid back. Kizzy was eleven years old when we lost Emma and twelve when Solei arrived. Again she welcomed the new puppy allowing her to nestle up to her although she showed her displeasure when Solei bit her tail!

Kizzy was a remarkable Beardie: such a comedian, giving us lots of laughs. Sadly we said goodbye to her just into her fifteenth year.

Joyce Ives

EMMA was our second Beardie, fawn in colour. She was a handful, a typical Beardie, and I was grateful to have had Kizzy first. If it had been the other way round I would have struggled. A totally loyal girl, when out walking she would return to my side if a man approached us in the woods without a canine companion.

I was talked into showing her as she was well-made and very feminine. Unfortunately, me being a novice I did not realise that fawns were frowned upon in the ring, but we did quite well at Open Shows.

Emma bounced her way through several years enjoying walking holidays on Dartmoor with Kizzy, her best buddy. On one of these holidays in 1992 we noticed her lack of exuberance and a month later, aged five, she was diagnosed with Addison's Disease. With medication and close monitoring, I managed to keep on top of each crisis. When she was not well, she climbed on our laps for warmth.

At the end of September 1996 during one of our walking holidays, she wasn't well and two weeks later she was diagnosed with a mass on her spleen. Our vet agreed she should be allowed to pass over the Rainbow Bridge.

I will never forget how grateful she was to me as I strove to make her comfortable each time she had an Addison's crisis. We could read each other's minds.

Joyce Ives

MUFFIN. Our third Beardie girl, slate in colour, joined us and Emma tolerated her – just – but after Muffin's canine mum came to stay, she showed Emma how to play with her, they then became great friends. Muffin was introduced to the show ring and she loved 'strutting her stuff' and was quite successful.

At eight years old Muffin was diagnosed with an enlarged heart and took medication for the rest of her life. I retired her from the show ring as was told she only had a short time to live!

Muffin always enjoyed attending the Spring Frolic, Strawberry Tea and The Tramp's Tuck In and would wander around saying hello to everyone and their Beardies and of course loved all our walking holidays.

She took in her stride our move in 2004 and was thankful there were no stairs to climb. We had two walking holidays that year, the second one she found more difficult and we eased back a little. 2006 we holidayed with friends and Muffin still surprised us in keeping up, although needed our help quite often as the area was hilly.

As the months passed, Muffin was walked on her own as she only wanted to use her energy to relieve herself. I found her one morning lying on her side motionless. She had had a stroke.

I know you shouldn't have favourites but Muffin was ours, she was such a sweet gentle girl; when on the move, she always carried a dolly I had knitted in her soft mouth, a substitute for the puppies she never had. We were grateful that the diagnosis of a short life was wrong and when we lost her she was a month into her sixteenth year.

Joyce Ives

SOLEI was quite a pickle and our only Beardie that tended to chew everything in sight. Bones were not enough and my glasses and the fireside chair also got her attention!

I took Solei away to Devon for a week's holiday with my friend Barbara and her dog Annie. We were only allowed to take two dogs and Solei was chosen as my husband preferred to look after Kizzy and Muffin, as they were no trouble!

Solei's showing career was short-lived, as she was totally bored, so she became our retirement dog. Also the cost of entering and driving to shows had increased tremendously. Muffin and Solei got on well together although Solei was my most sensitive Beardie and suffered with health problems.

When Muffin passed over the Rainbow Bridge, Solei was devastated and she realised Muffin wasn't coming back. She lay down in the bathroom and gave a long, awful-sounding, low, guttural howl. From then on, she wouldn't let us out of her sight and couldn't be left on her own, as she barked and hyperventilated. Her health over the years deteriorated: an underactive thyroid gland, and lastly liver problems.

Our Beardies are waiting over the Rainbow Bridge for us so we can all happily be reunited.

Joyce Ives

Lightning Source UK Ltd.
Milton Keynes UK
UKHW05f0509200918
329179UK00009B/122/P